TWICE BORN

A Book of Conversion Stories

Compiled and Edited by
NORMAN A. WINGERT, M. A.
Missionary to Japan

ZONDERVAN PUBLISHING HOUSE
Grand Rapids, Michigan

Printed in the United States of America

Foreword

It has been computed that if the first convert to Christianity had won one soul within a year, and that one another, with each new convert winning one a year, the whole world would have become Christian within thirty-two years.

But this has not been done. There are still millions to be converted.

Some are called to preach, but all are called to witness. After all, there is nothing as effective as a personal testimony. Three times the story of Paul's conversion is related in the New Testament. His enemies did their best to answer his arguments but they never did succeed in explaining the miraculous change in his life. His testimony was unanswerable.

The stories in this book are true. They actually took place. These people were born again. They had a personal experience with Jesus Christ. They know whereof they speak, for they were there when it happened. No one can contradict them. Their testimony is, "Once I was blind; now I see!" Where, then, is there any room for argument?

Now then the same Christ who did it for them can also do it for others. That is why the author has brought together the stories in this book. His first book of conversion stories entitled, *I Was Born Again*, now in its third edition, has been used to convince many of the ever-present power of God to save. It is the kind of testimony we need today, and I am glad my good friend, Norman A. Wingert, with whom I traveled in Europe, has compiled the volume which you now hold in your hand.

This book emphasizes above all the necessity of decision. We can not drift into the Christian life; we must be born into it. A decision must be made. The command, "Choose you this day," characterizes every page. Here are men and women out of every rank and file in life—good and bad, rich and poor, high and low—but every one of them has become a Christian through a deliberate choice of Christ as Savior. May these testimonies encourage others to make this all-important choice.

Oswald J. Smith, Litt. D.

The Peoples Church
Toronto, Canada

Introduction

Christian witnessing is a chain reaction. Ever since Jesus said to His disciples, "Ye are my witnesses," the good news of what God can do has been passed from mouth to mouth down to the present day.

Release of the spiritual dynamic in one heart touches off the explosion of a miracle in a second heart, and thus does the chain of spiritual new-birth continue from generation to generation.

One soul finds forgiveness and freedom and fellowship in faith in Christ, and he says to his neighbor, "O come and taste that the Lord is good." His neighbor comes and sees, and then, in turn, says to *his* neighbor, "O come and taste that the Lord is good."

It is unnatural and it is criminal to refuse help to a dying man. He who refrains from passing along the good news of how to be cured of a dread disease either has not himself experienced the full potency of the cure, or has not been aware of the certainty of its fatal end. We who have been saved from the power and penalty of sin *must* speak of that which we have heard and experienced, so that others, too, may know how to find healing and forgiveness.

Today more than ever the world wants to hear the genuine Christian witness. Sham and pretenses and false testimonies are out, but simple, sincere statements of the transforming power of God in individual lives still attract attentive ears.

The favorable reception of my first book of conversion stories is one indication of the readiness of the public to give an ear to sincere Christian testimonies. *I Was Born Again* has had three large printings and has been adopted by three book-of-the-month clubs.

The second volume of conversion stories is but a continuation of the first. The idea back of both books has been a very simple one—to provide a medium by which those who have been redeemed of the Lord can say so.

I have met personally most of the people whose testimonies you are about to read. They are normal and intelligent folk, and the stories which they relate are not figments and fancies of the imagination but are actual, factual experiences.

I invite you, reader, to give these witnesses a sympathetic hearing. Some of you, I know, will thrill to the stories and will say, "I know what he is talking about for I have had the same experience." Others of you who are still carrying your own heavy burdens may feel a deepening desire to become personally acquainted with Him who said, "Come unto me all ye that labor and are heavy laden and I will give you rest." You, too, will have the thrill of your life the moment you come to Him in deepest sincerity and repentance and hear Him say, "Be of good cheer, thy sins are forgiven thee."

My sincere thanks are due to everyone who has contributed to the making of this book, including Miss Mary Stoner who typed the manuscript and offered helpful suggestions.

Norman A. Wingert

Taylor University
Upland, Indiana

CONTENTS

Jesus answered, Verily, verily, I say unto thee, Except a man be born of water and of the Spirit, he cannot enter into the kingdom of God. That which is born of the flesh is flesh; and that which is born of the Spirit is spirit.

Marvel not that I said unto thee, Ye must be born again.

John 3:5-7

THE CONVERSION STORIES

1　　　　　**CALLING YOUTH TO CHRIST**

BILLY GRAHAM'S TESTIMONY

Many of you have experienced the thrill of flying above the storm and clouds and I am sure that you, on many occasions, have thought, as I have, how that experience is paralleled in our spiritual lives. Wherever I go, young people have virtually the same problems, most of which revolve around two or three pivots. Christian young people often ask me, "How can I get the joy and thrill of Christian living that you have been talking about? I have *not* been living above the clouds: I have been living in the valleys. I am miserable in my Christian experience." A young worldling said to me the other day, "You Christians seem to have a religion that makes you miserable. You are like a man with a headache. He does not want to get rid of his head, but it hurts him to keep it. You cannot expect outsiders to seek anything so unfavorable!"

Is that true in your life? Have you been living an *up and down experience?* I am convinced that it is possible for young people to have lives of inward rest and outward victory. It is your birthright. Many of you can remember the shout of triumph your soul gave when you first met Jesus Christ! How sure you were of victory then! How easy it seemed to be more than a conqueror through Him that loved you! Under the leadership of such a general you can never be foiled in battle, yet how different has been the experience of many of you! Your victories have been few and fleeting, your defeats many and disastrous. You have not lived as you think a Christian ought to live. Perhaps you have a good understanding of doctrinal truths and you know a few Scripture verses and have made a study of the Bible; possibly you believe in Christ, you talk about Him and you know you are saved; but somehow there is something wrong. In the very depths of your heart and soul you realize that your experience is not a scriptural experience. Many of you have given up in despair and have said, "It is impossible. All I can expect is an alternate life of victory and despair. I must always live in the valley! I can never enjoy the sunshine of the sunny mountain slopes! It is impossible always to fly above the clouds." Is that your experience?

There are three words that I want to use which may touch upon the secret of your failure. You will find them in the writings of Paul to young Timothy.

They are: *retreat; stand; advance.* First and Second Timothy are good books for any Christian young person to read and study. Timothy was a young man, very much like some of you. He faced the same temptations, the same trials, had the same burdens and the same problems that you have. He was a man of like passions. Timothy had been converted at an early age and answered the call to preach the Gospel of Jesus Christ, which is the greatest challenge and call that any young man can have.

I. RETREAT

In the sixth chapter of First Timothy we find in the eleventh verse that Paul says this: "But thou, O man of God, flee these things; and follow after righteousness, godliness, faith, love, patience, meekness."

I think that General Timishinko of Russia will probably go down in history as the world's greatest leader of strategic retreat. You will remember that he led the armies of Russia back from the Polish border all the way to Stalingrad and kept them intact until the time came for the forward move that carried the great Russian Bear to the heart of Berlin.

There comes a time in our lives when God says, "Run! Flee! Get Away! Leave it alone! Have nothing to do with it! Avoid it!" Paul was giving this advice to young Timothy.

Let us give attention to some of the things which he was anxious that young Timothy should avoid. Notice that he mentions—

Pride

The root of all sin is pride. Perhaps the greatest sin that has crept into the lives of Christians is the sin of pride. No young person can expect victory and inward rest until the capital *I* has been conquered. God commands us to "humble ourselves." We are never told to pray for humility! That is our job! If we are to live above the clouds, the sin of pride will have to be confessed and forsaken. It is deadlier than the poison of a rattlesnake. It stunts, stifles, weakens and destroys Christian victory.

When I was a student at Wheaton College a great revival swept our campus. Dr. Harold Warren was the human instrument, but it was the Holy Spirit who did the job. From ten o'clock in the morning until eleven at night on two successive days, classes and meals were

13

forgotten as students confessed their sins and God took over. The sin that was confessed most often publicly and privately was the sin of pride. Students, staff and faculty alike realized that this awful sin was ruining their individual victory with God. If that is your sin, confess it today and be rid of it.

Strife

This is the next thing from which Paul urges young Timothy to flee. Do you get angry easily? Are you impatient? Are you irritable? Do little things vex and annoy? Are there uprisings within? Do you lose your temper? Does wrath hold you at times in its grip? All of these things engender strife. God calls it sin! Many Christian homes where I am entertained are filled with strife. The father and the mother are continually bickering and arguing. The children, instead of being well disciplined, argue with their parents. The sweet aroma of Christian love is weakened. God says that such strife is sin. Let us confess and forsake it.

Envy

This is the green-eyed monster that has wrecked so many young Christians. It creeps in unexpectedly and slays us before we know it. God says (Prov. 6:34), "For jealousy is the rage of a man: therefore he will not spare in the day of vengeance." Some young people are jealous because others are more handsome and more beautiful than they; jealous because others can play the piano and they cannot; jealous because the pastor shakes hands more cordially with others than with them. These things can ruin your Christian experience and keep you in the valley of gloomy defeat. "But thou, O man of God, flee these things." Avoid jealousy.

Railing

Railing simply means old-fashioned gossiping, talking about your neighbors without foundation for what you have to say. It is sin. Scripture says, "Be swift to hear, slow to speak" (Jas. 1:19); "The tongue is a fire, a world of iniquity . . . and it is set on fire of hell" (Jas. 3:6). Your tongue is one of the smallest members of your body, yet it is more powerful and deadly than an atomic bomb. Let us pray more for our friends—and talk less! Everywhere I go someone wants to take me aside and tell me an evil story about some Christian worker. I hate it! I don't want to hear it! Ninety per cent of the stories that go around about men of God are untrue. Let us confess our sin. Let us confess these filthy communications. They grieve the Holy Spirit.

Evil Surmising

The searchlight of the Holy Spirit goes deeper than the tongue. It exposes even the thinking of our minds and hearts! Paul says, "Timothy, avoid thinking evil about others!" Think the best of everyone! If you follow this rule in your Christian experience you will find your life cleaner, happier and more vibrant. Gossiping and evil surmising can become habits that stunt our Christian growth and development.

The Love of Money

Paul mentions in the tenth verse of the sixth chapter of First Timothy "the love of money." Many young Christians have been caught in this subtle trap of Satan. You say, "But I have no money to love." I have talked with many people who did not make five dollars a week, but the love of money was keeping them from living victorious lives in Christ. Christ demands the prominent

15

place! He demands leadership! Striving after money and this world's goods is called sin!

Youthful Lusts

Writing to Timothy on another occasion, Paul warns him to flee something else: "Flee also youthful lusts" (II Tim. 2:22). Young men and women, lust is a deadly thing. Every outward immoral sin begins with a thought. Guard your thoughts. Keep them clean. Keep them pure. Purpose in your heart that you will not defile yourself. Don't let your eyes look upon that which grieves the Holy Spirit.

Dr. V. R. Edman, president of Wheaton College, said something in chapel one day which I shall never forget: "The first look is not sin. It is the second look!" You may be unable to help the first look, but watch and guard that second look. "Flee youthful lusts."

II. Stand

The sun was shining in a clear blue sky. Semitropical Pasadena was filled with an air of excitement. It was not just an ordinary holiday. It was the one big day of the year when the eyes of the sports world turned to this Los Angeles suburb. Palm trees, orange groves, balmy breezes and the Rose Bowl game were going to make New Year's Day southern California's "big day." T. W. Wilson and I had been given "hard to get" tickets by Miss Henrietta Mears, "The Lady" at Hollywood's First Presbyterian Church. We made our way to Section D, seats 21 and 22. Soon we were shouting, laughing, eating peanuts and having a good time. T. W. and I, being true Southerners, were loyal to Alabama's Crimson Tide. By the end of the first quarter it was apparent that it was Alabama all the way. As the Tide neared the Southern

California goal line, the cheering students of California broke out in this chant: "Hold that line! Hold that line!" As I watched that scene so filled with tenseness and excitement it seemed that I could see a spiritual drama being enacted. I could see myself before "so great a cloud of witnesses" and being tempted by Satan while the great witnesses of the past who had lived for and died in this same arena were shouting to me, "Hold the line. Don't yield. Stand, and having done all, stand!"

I am sure that many of you, when just about to yield or compromise in your Christian lives, have heard the still, small voice of God saying, "Hold that line. Don't yield to Satan's subtle temptations, 'that ye may be able to stand against the wiles of the devil' " (Eph. 6:11). Again God has said, "Watch ye, stand fast in the faith, quit you like men, be strong" (I Cor. 16:13) or again, in Galatians 5:1, "Stand fast therefore in the liberty wherewith Christ hath made us free."

Yield everything to Him! The greatest thing you must yield is yourself, because the greatest burden one has to carry in life is self—his daily living, his failings, his special weaknesses and temptations, his peculiar temperament, his inward affairs of every kind. You must hand all these to God and leave them there. He demands that you surrender your reputation, your Christian work, your love affairs, your houses, your children, your business, your servants—everything, whether inward or outward—to Him. Not only must you commit the things of the future but more difficult still, you must commit the present to Him. If you have committed your problems to the Lord, forget them. Don't worry about them. Most people take their burdens, troubles and sins to Him,

17

but they bring them away with them again and are as worried and unhappy as before.

God will expect no less than *all*. We must confess with our mouths the Lord Jesus Christ. He demands Lordship. Thus, when you are entirely yielded to Him, He fills you with His Spirit, and His powerful dynamo called the Holy Spirit will enable you to stand against every onslaught of Satan. "When thou goest out to battle against thine enemies, and seest horses, and chariots, and a people more than thou, be not afraid of them: for the Lord thy God is with thee, which brought thee up out of the land of Egypt" (Deut. 20:1).

It is not a battle with flesh and blood; it is a spiritual battle against principalities, against powers, against rulers of the darkness of this world, against spiritual wickedness in high places. The Holy Spirit is absolutely the only one who can give you the ability to "hold the line." Are you holding? Are you standing? Only as you "stand" against every attack can you say you are living above the clouds in glorious sunlight on the mountain slopes of God's love, peace, joy, happiness and pleasure. "In thy presence is fulness of joy; at thy right hand are pleasures forevermore."

III. ADVANCE

When I was seven my father bought me my first bicycle. I had never ridden one. Patiently my family and friends tried to teach me the art of cycling. I soon found that there was one thing that I must do if I was to stay on the bicycle: keep moving forward. If I ceased to go forward I would fall and hurt myself. So it is in the Christian life. Paul told Timothy not only to endure hardness as a good soldier but to "strive" for masteries. Peter said, "But grow in grace, and in the knowledge of our Lord and Saviour Jesus Christ (II Pet. 3:18).

You can never live this glorious life on the highest plane unless you are continually growing and moving forward. If you are not closer to Christ and more mature spiritually today than at any time in your Christian experience, there is something wrong with your life. You should be closer to Him today, heart, soul and body, than at any time in your life. There should be a constant growth.

John spoke of fathers, young men and little children (I John 2:13). He was speaking of spiritually mature men—young men who were growing but who had not reached spiritual maturity—and babes in Christ. There are degrees of spiritual growth. You cannot grow in justification; there is no development in the standing of your relationship with God.

You ask, "How can I grow? How can I advance? How can I move forward?" *First: Bible reading:* "Desire the sincere milk of the word, that ye may grow thereby" (I Pet. 2:2). Read it! Study it! Meditate on it! Memorize it! Ninety per cent of the Christian's difficulties and troubles are caused by a lack of reading and studying the Word. Do not be content to skim through a chapter merely to satisfy your conscience. Hide the Word of God in your heart. A little portion well masticated is of greater spiritual value to your soul than a lengthy portion scanned hurriedly. Do not be discouraged because you cannot understand it all. The greatest theologians have had to say, "The half has not been told." However, the Holy Spirit will make hard passages plain to you, and the Word will become a living reality in your heart.

19

Prayer

The enemy is attacking. We need to fortify our prayer lives. Prayer is the Christian's greatest weapon. Young people, you cannot get along without it. You can never live the life above the clouds without being instant in prayer in season and out of season. This doesn't mean that the only time you can pray is when you are alone or hidden in a private closet. You have access to the throne room at any moment of the day. You are the child of a King. It is your royal privilege to talk with your Father. He is interested in every detail of your life. The little heartaches, burdens and troubles that nobody else knows about—in these He is keenly interested. He has numbered the hairs of your head. He wants to help you with even the most simple things that you would ordinarily not bother anyone about. God is interested. Let Him bear your burdens. Let Him solve your problems. Learn to pray victoriously. Such prayer is necessary for spiritual growth.

Witnessing

God's purpose for you and me after we have been converted is that we be witnesses to His saving grace and power. Are you a daily and constant witness? Are you one of God's minutemen? Are you a commando for Christ? He expects you to witness at every given opportunity. "Whosoever therefore shall confess me before men," Christ said, "him will I confess also before my Father which is in heaven."

Remember, we are sowing seed. Some indeed may fall on beaten paths and some among thorns, but it is our business to keep on sowing. We are not to stop sowing because some of the soil looks unpromising.

We are holding a light. We are to let it shine though it may seem but a twinkling candle in a world of blackness. It is our business to let it shine.

We are blowing a trumpet. In the din and noise of battle the sound of our little trumpet may seem to be lost, but we must keep sounding the alarm to those who are in danger.

We are kindling a fire in this cold old world full of hatred and selfishness. Our little blaze may seem to be unavailing, but we must keep our fire burning.

We are striking with a hammer. The blows may seem only to jar our hands as we strike, but we are to keep on hammering.

We are using a sword. The first or second thrust of our sword may be evaded and all of our efforts at striking deep into the enemy may seem hopeless, but we are to keep wielding our sword. It is the sword of the Spirit.

We have bread for a hungry world. The people may seem to be so busy feeding on other things that they will not accept the Bread of Life, but we must keep on giving it, offering it to the souls of men.

We have water for famishing people. We must keep standing and crying out, "Ho, every one that thirsteth, come ye to the waters." We must persevere. We must never give up. Keep using the Word.

The seed will find some good soil and spring up and bear fruit, even thirty or sixty or an hundredfold. Somebody will hear the trumpet, even in the din and tumult, and will flee to the Refuge and be safe. The fire will kindle a sacred flame in some cold hearts and woo them to God. The hammer will break some hard hearts and make them contrite and yielded to God. The sword will pierce the armor of sin and cut away the self-satisfaction and the pride and open hearts to the Spirit of God. Some hungry men and women will take the Bread of Life and some famishing ones will find the Water of Life at our hands.

Let us as Christian young people declare the whole Word of God.

After that the Lord takes over, giving you the grace and strength you need. For my own part, I was saved, and saved well. *The Lord did the job!*

In closing, to clarify and emphasize this matter of "Retreat, Stand, Advance," I want to point out that the point at which you must begin is *your own personal salvation experience.*

* * *

2   **USHERED TO THE MERCY SEAT**

As President of Youth for Christ International, Dr. Robert A. Cook makes it the chief concern of his life and of the organization which he heads to lead men and women to Christ. Youth for Christ International is not a little responsible for modern spiritual awakenings in all parts of the world. It is synonymous with present-day mass evangelism. Dr. Billy Graham is Vice President of the organization.

Only God can estimate the number of unseen souls that accompanied "Bobby" Cook when his father usher-ed him forward to the altar that evening.

I was six when the Lord laid His hand on me. Seated beside my father in the very last row in a Christian and Missionary Alliance church in Cleveland, Ohio, I felt a strange turbulence in my soul as the pastor, Rev. H. E. Nelson, spoke of how one can be saved through faith in the Lord Jesus Christ. Young as I was, I knew there that evening that I should make this important decision.

A whispered conference with my father, who was head usher that evening, showed me that he was entirely sympathetic toward my making this decision. With his arms around me, he lead me forward to the place of prayer. And there, at God His Mercy Seat, the Heavenly Father heard a little boy's prayers and saw his tears, forgave his sins, and came into the opened door of his heart to stay forever.

From that day on, my father never ceased to give me encouragement and counsel from the Word of God, nurturing and watering the seed of eternal life that had been sown. I was encouraged to memorize Bible verses and to study various books of the Bible while still young. I have never gotten away from the benefits of these early practices; it has paid out in blessing and joy all my life.

I feel that, as so often happens to young people, there had to come to me a time of definite "selling out" to God. This took place in my later teens when in my own room I said a real "Yes" to God and turned the reins of my life over to Him.

What a joy it is to know the Lord Jesus Christ and to have the knowledge that His hand has been upon me throughout the ups and downs of all the past years. What a wonderful Savior He is!

* * *

3   **THERE IS A GOD, AND I'VE MET HIM**

R. Mabel Francis has been a missionary in Japan for forty years, and was interned there during the War. Mrs. Francis has been asked by the Government in

Japan to organize women's groups. In a short period she visited thirty such groups with as many as 1000 women present. "More and more it grows on me," she says, "that the hour for revival in Japan has come."

In World War Two, Japanese youth found themselves moving along at such an accelerating tempo that the unexpected signing of the Armistice was like a brake on the wheel, and bewildering in its suddenness. Not knowing how to interpret defeat or the strange tearing down of all that had been previously taught them, the young people of Japan were smitten with confusion.

One youth, a man of Christian parents who was about to be graduated from Teacher's Normal College, was stunned by the defeat and dazed by the contradiction of it all. Upon meeting the missionary he firmly declared, "I do not want to hear anything about religion. Please don't talk to me about it. I have decided to become an atheist, and that is final."

I complied with his request not to talk to him about religion, but I did talk to God about the young man, in fervent prayer.

Meanwhile the youth was saying to himself, "If I am to put up a profession as an atheist, to be consistent I must produce as good character as these Christians." But his atheism did not produce the equivalent to Christian character. As the days passed he not only found his standards slipping, but his daily life and conduct seemed, as he said later, "to be crumbling at the base."

One night he was walking by the seaside in great distress. He sat down to think through his dilemma, but the more he thought, the greater became his distress. He saw how his whole life was failing. He fell on his face in the sand, and cried out in his agony, "There must be a God; I must have a God!" Involuntarily he started confessing aloud the blackness and sin of his proud heart.

All at once it seemed to him as if it became light— as light as day—and a sweet sense of forgiveness of sin came over him. Leaping up from the sand he began to praise God. The praises increased, flowed on and on until, not knowing how further to express this newfound joy, he stripped off his kimona, dashed into the sea, looked up to heaven and cried, "O God, I have found You! I have found You!"

The next morning, very early, he bounded into the front entrance of the mission home. "I see it!" he exclaimed, "I see it! Oh, there *is* a God, *and I've met Him!*"

After a time of praise and of confirming his faith in the Word of God, he went back to his school to tell them about the wonderful God he met that morning on the seashore.

* * *

4   **NOW I KNOW WHERE I'M GOING**

Holder of the National Intercollegiate Boxing championship in 1944, a past president of the student body and graduate of the University of Virginia, Robert V. Finley became one of the founding staff members of Inter-Varsity Christian Fellowship.

Of the experience which he and Bob Pierce had in Korea just prior to the outbreak of war there in June, 1950, Finley says that he saw revival come to Korea: saw more than twenty-five thousand persons profess to accept Christ as Savior within six weeks; saw more than four thousand persons daily at five o'clock morning prayer meetings; saw hundreds continue all night in prayer for days on end; saw crowds up to seventy-five thousand come together to hear the gospel; saw the Holy Spirit at work.

The story of his conversion will appeal strongly to that large group of young people for whom life has no significant meaning.

Life has meaning for me.

There is a purpose in life that makes every moment worthwhile and enjoyable. Life is not just a series of ups and downs, joys and sorrows, pains and pleasures thrown together in a humdrum existence. No! Not any more, at least.

There was a time when living on this earth was sheer boredom for me. It seemed to be a meaningless moment between two blank eternities—here today and gone tomorrow.

But suddenly, a few years ago, Something entered my life to bring order out of chaos, peace out of conflict, harmony out of discord. Since then every aspect of life has become meaningful. It makes sense. I know where I came from, why I am here, and where I am going.

That *Something* which entered my life was a *Person*; not just an ordinary person, but the King of kings, the Lord of lords, the Creator of heaven and earth, the very Personification of life and reason, the only wise God, our Lord and Savior Jesus Christ. Now, "to me to live is Christ."

Let me tell you how it happened.

As a child growing up on a farm in Virginia, I became extremely curious to know the Infinite Rationality behind the laws of nature. I knew well that what we ignorantly called *Mother Nature* was really the handiwork of Almighty God. I could not doubt the existence of God even if I tried. But the thing that bothered me was that I couldn't see God. To know that He existed was not enough; I wanted to get in touch with Him. Once when I narrowly escaped death I became fearful lest I should die before I had made this contact with my Maker. I had come to love life, and down in my heart of hearts I knew that it would have been better never to have lived than to live and die without ever knowing the purpose of existence or the Person responsible for it.

My parents were church members and they took me frequently to Sunday School and worship services. At the age of fifteen I affiliated with their church. But to my dismay I found there no help in my search for God. In Sunday School I learned a few moral platitudes, and in church the minister talked about solving current social problems; but I heard never a word about how to know God. Soon I lost interest in church attendance because the particular church I attended failed to give me what my soul was seeking.

I must say, however, that I am indebted to my parents and to my church for one thing that proved to be a turning point in my life; from them I learned that one might obtain information about God from the Bible. Accordingly I began to read the Word of God at odd moments during my senior year in high school, and I knew instinctively that this was the real source of information about God. But still I did not come to know Him in a personal way.

Graduation time came, followed by a summer of dull and drab drudgery on the farm. Life was meaningless. I rebelled against it. If only I could get away from the farm, see the world, and have fun, I would be happy, I thought. So one summer night, while all were asleep, I slipped out of the house and ran away from home. I traveled far and wide, earning my support by doing odd jobs. As winter approached I made my way to Florida and settled down to a good job in Miami. Soon I had all the things which I had hoped might bring happiness —money, friends, pleasure. But still life continued to be empty. And more depressing still, I discovered that my friends in Miami Beach who had the most money were more miserable than even I.

In desperation I began once more to read the Bible. But as I read it my misery increased. It told me of the laws of God which I had broken. It told me of the wrath of God upon sin which I knew I justly deserved. I felt that there was no hope for me. I was a guilty sinner doomed to eternal hell. I lay awake nights worrying. I walked the streets, unable to rest. I felt the awful emptiness of a life without God closing in to smother out my very existence. I must find God or lose my mind. Most of my friends seemed already to have lost their minds without realizing it.

Then God came to my rescue. He gave me some new friends to whom He had given a new mind. The first was a young man who had just graduated from a Bible school in New York. God brought him to Miami and put him in a hotel just across the street from where I stayed. In providence we met, and the young man talked to me about his relationship to God. He talked of having been saved, of having been born again, of having begun life all over anew. He took me to several churches— vastly different from my home church—where I met other young people who had had the same experience. I knew at once that these young people had found the answer to the riddle of life which had puzzled me so long.

From my associations with these new-found friends, from the sermons I heard in their churches, and from a Bible teacher whose classes I attended, I was led a step further in my understanding of the Bible. I came face to face with the Person of our blessed Savior in all of His deity and glory. Up to this time I had regarded Jesus merely as a teacher, an exponent of the Law of God. His legal teachings and His perfect example had condemned me in the sight of a Holy God. But now I came to realize that He was more than a teacher—He was a *Savior*. He had paid in my place the death penalty which my sins deserved, so that now I could be accepted in the sight of God as if I had never sinned.

On my soul fell the full impact of this truth. It was the best news I had ever heard. I *knew* that it was true, and by faith I claimed His death as a sacrifice for my sins. Immediately my burden was lifted, my guilt was gone, and my life was flooded with the joy and peace that can come only to one who has been reconciled to God. I was born again.

Now for the first time I really began to live. Instead of enduring a meaningless existence, I entered into all the joys of eternal life. I know without a doubt I am a

29

child of God. I know I shall never die. I know I shall
enjoy the glory of His fellowship forever and forever.

I know now where I am going.

* * *

5   **HE SET THE BIRDS FREE**

By Aristide Malinverni

"I absolve thee."

These words I repeated no less than fifty thousand
times during my priesthood as I raised my hand over
the heads of the penitents. There were days when I was
for five or six hours continually in the confessional box.

But a still, small voice was protesting to my conscience, Where did you get this tremendous authority?
Are you a god who can forgive sins? If you are bound
in your own sins, how can you expect to loose the sins
of the people? Don't you see that you are a blasphemer?

In this way God was speaking to my soul in the very
moment when I was vainly trying to usurp His authority.

Despite these inner misgivings, I continued to give
blind adherence to the faith and practice of the Roman
Church. I served the "holy" Church as priest, as teacher
in a seminary, and as editor of a Roman Catholic news-
paper in Italy.

But after many years of long and careful reflection,
I finally reached the point where I no longer believed
in the fundamental doctrines of the Roman Church. How
could I longer teach others what I myself did not
believe?

For a whole year the struggle went on between my
awakened conscience and my personal interest; you see,
I had a very lucrative position in the Roman Church,

and my prospect for future honors and financial advancement was very bright.

The break finally came. I left my parish and the Roman Church, and, after unspeakable persecutions in Italy from my former friends and associates, I left my country to come to this blessed land of America where God was waiting to give me the fullness of His light and grace.

In America I found myself a Protestant. I was intellectually changed. I even developed a deep-seated hatred against the superstition and errors of the Catholic Church. But I was not yet born again. The creed was changed, but not the heart.

A year later, that, too, happened. While I was listening to a Salvation Army speaker on Fourteenth Street, New York City, I felt the Spirit of God speaking to me with such profound accents that I was constrained to go forward and kneel at the mercy seat. How long I knelt, I can not tell.

And then, at the very moment of my full surrender, a clear vision of the crucified Jesus was displayed before my astonished eyes and worshipful soul. From the lips of Jesus I heard with perfect assurance the sweet words, "Thy sins are forgiven." The chains of hatred fell off and my heart was made free.

Walking in the streets of a city one day, I was attracted to some cages containing birds that were exposed for sale. I suddenly stopped and looked on them intently. I saw that the poor birds ruffled their sunny plumage on the wires and struggled to be free.

Wistfully and sadly I looked again and again on these captives till tears started in my eyes. Turning to their owner, I asked the price of one, paid it, opened the door and set the prisoner free. And thus I did with captive after captive, until every bird was away soaring to the skies and singing on the wings of liberty.

The crowd around me stared and stood amazed. They thought me mad. Plainly they wanted an explanation for such unusual doings.

"I was once myself a captive," I said to the curious group, "but Christ has set me free; you see, I know the sweets of liberty."

* * *

6   I SEARCHED ALL MY LIFE

Art Atwell need not be introduced to television fans. He used to be a weekly visitor in West Coast homes. His story shows clearly how unsatisfactory is even the highest achievement if Christ is left out.

My wife and I were married young, and the path that stretched ahead looked long and rosy. Our plans for a career were already laid. I had given a passing thought to the ministry just before graduating from college but, blaming that trend of thinking on my imagination, I quickly eliminated it as a consideration for a career and focused my attention on the one great passion of my life—my trumpet. On my trumpet our success was to depend; everything else was to be secondary. I would practice, practice, practice, I said, and progress from band to better band until eventually I would achieve perfection and success and—complete happiness.

We went ahead according to plans. Following college, I taught school for a year. Then, leaving my wife to stay with my folks, I set out for San Francisco to find an opening in music. There I landed my first job in the Don Kay orchestra.

"Honey," I wrote to my wife as I invited her to join me, "we've really got it! It isn't the best job yet, but it's good enough. I can practice hard, and I can make enough so that we can get ahead and have just the life we want."

About a year later, Henry Busse's orchestra and ours had simultaneous engagements in Dayton, Ohio. We were playing in the Biltmore hotel and they, a theatre engagement. Their director would come to the hotel for dinner after his last performance. Each evening for two weeks I wanted to ask him for a place on his orchestra, but always my nerve failed me, and the only result was hard practice the next day for my anticipated new job. When I finally did ask him, on the very last night, it turned out that Busse had me spotted and was just waiting for me to ask him so he could get me at a cheaper price—which he did.

Despite this "gyp," the job paid what was then a fabulous salary. I'll never forget how happy we were that first night. With tears of joy we said, "Boy, now we've really got the life we want; besides, it's a step to something even higher."

The year spent with Busse's orchestra was, however, not as ideal as we had pictured it. Reluctantly I observed that something was lacking. Everybody seemed to be searching for something. They would say, "Have you tried this?" or "Have you tried that?" They were groping as though in the dark. But wife and I rationalized the whole situation; we said that the dissatisfaction

33

which we saw on every hand was due to the fact that everybody was too busy. Living in hotels, eating at restaurants, traveling as much as five hundred miles a day, signing autographs (with a smile, of course!) for the scores of admirers around the bandstand, and playing a full program into the wee hours of the morning, was indeed a strenuous life. Often I would think to myself as I wrote my name beside those of other "big shots," "What in the world do you want my autograph for, when it is you who is to be envied for your opportunity of living a normal life?"

So we thought that life would be perfect if only we did not have to travel.

Back in San Francisco again, I learned of a vacancy in the Golden Gate theatre there. In line with our search for the ideal and perfectly happy life, I tried out and got the job. "Honey," I said that evening, "now our worries are over; I got the life we want and now we're going to live in one place. We don't have to live in hotels now, and we can be normal people."

Before the curtain went up the first night, I knew there was something wrong here too. "Quick, one last drink," they said as the five-minute signal flashed. I thought, "What's the need for so much stimulant? This is normal business. We are now living a normal, happy life!" I found again that everybody was searching for something.

Then the War came on, and I went with the Phil Harris band in the maritime service. There was excitement and adventure, but little peace of mind.

Upon release from service, my wife and I came to Hollywood. "Now, Honey, we are where we want to be," I said; and I spent hours in practicing for a coveted position with the National Broadcasting Company Staff orchestra. I finally tried out and got the job.

And again I exclaimed, "We've really got it now, *a permanent job in Hollywood!*"

But as you can guess, disillusionment came again; the people there were searching too. Again I rationalized as to why so many people were searching and why I had not yet found peace in my heart. It is, I thought, because musicians are under such terrific strain. A good trumpet player dare not miss a note, for if he does someone else will get his job; and I would go home evenings exhausted from the nervous strain. I thought that if only I could work less hours, then the strain would not be so great, and I could be perfectly happy. I said to my wife, "The job I really want is in the studios."

So one day I heard of an opening, and I tried out for the RKO Staff orchestra in Hollywood. I got the job. And when I came home I said, "Honey, we've reached the top rung of the ladder; now there's no excuse to worry about anything."

And there really wasn't!—at least when viewed from the human angle. The job paid the biggest salary I had yet received, and we worked only a few hours a week. I would call up at the beginning of the week and ask, "When do we work?" and they would say, "Monday afternoon and Thursday night." The rest of the time we had to ourselves, and I was free to book engagements for myself. I made much extra money for I was booked almost every night. Here, then, was the pinnacle of my earlier dreams: a polished trumpet player earning top money! Then something came into my life to "spoil" this ideal setup.

"This is Jimmy Borsen," a voice said over the telephone one evening. "Will you be busy Sunday night?"

I pulled out my date book and said, "No, I don't believe I will."

"I am the musical director at Angelus Temple," the voice continued. "Would you come over and play . . . ?"

"Sorry," I interrupted; "but I find that after all I do have an engagement," and quickly hung up. I heaved a sigh of relief and thought, "Boy, that was a close call; I'm not playing in any church!"

This Jimmy Borsen called several times more, and I always gave him the same answer. Then one day he reversed his tactics. I do not say that he disguised his voice, but at least I didn't recognize that it was he when a voice said, "Are you busy Sunday evening?"

I replied, "No."

"This is Jimmy Borsen. Will you play . . . ?"

I did play that next Sunday evening in the Angelus Temple orchestra. It was my first time in twelve years inside a church. Everything seemed so strange, so amusing. "There's something altogether different down there," I told my wife when I went home.

That "something different" caused me to go back again. Soon I found myself there every week, and as the weeks went on I began to feel a hungering and a yearning in my heart.

Meanwhile I had joined Spade Cooley's orchestra and made my debut in television. This was bringing us in extra money which together with the income from the Studio orchestra and my private engagements added up to the handsomest salary in our lives. Despite this, that hunger for something that satisfies was increasing. Said I to myself, "I'm busy, I'm making money, yet there is no peace in our hearts; I don't know what else to expect from the world."

As I said, I was playing in the Temple orchestra every Sunday night. Usually, however, I would leave the service just before the sermon in order to play at a Jewish wedding, for I was on several bands that played only at weddings. On my way, I would listen to the sermon by radio. I would listen right up to the start of our program just so I could hear more of the sermon. The hunger was deepening.

One day I was talking with one of the boys of the Studio Orchestra. He said, "Art, you'd better be careful. I understand that down there you don't have to use any reasoning with the Bible; you don't have to use your intelligence at all; you just believe the whole thing. You'd better look out, because an intelligent man can't do that." I said, "OK, I'll watch it; I'll be careful." It seemed logical to me. I had never read the Bible, but this fellow was my boss; he was a band leader, and band leaders always know more than the musician.

The next week — the Lord planned this for me — Chaplain Rushtoi spoke in the message about people who do not believe the Bible. He said that the man who does not believe the Bible is an extreme egotist, for he is putting his own opinions above the Word of God, the Word which has stood for centuries.

That made sense to me too, so when I got to the job, I said to this fellow, "You know, the man who claims he doesn't believe the Bible is a pretty big egotist because he is putting his own opinion above the Word of God. "Art," he said, "I know a musician who went to Angelus Temple, and he's still there."

It was about that time that the people in the Temple band started to pray for me. They were "doublecross-ing" me, although I did not know it at the time. I would catch myself asking questions I did not mean to ask, and that would tip my hand that I needed salvation. I began to see that these people had the thing I was hunting for.

One evening some of these friends prayed with me in the band room. It was the first time in many years that I had prayed and that I had heard someone praying for me. I had tears in my eyes, and they said to me, "Art, will you give your heart to the Lord?" I said, "No, I can't do it." They said, "Art, what is it? Is it money?" I said, "No, it isn't money; I'm making money and I'm not happy." They asked, "Is it pride?" I said, "No, it's not pride. I'm just ashamed to make another promise, for years ago I lied to the Lord and I don't want to do it again."

Well, by this time I had a real need, and I was pray-ing about it up in the hills the next day as I was practicing. The Lord came to me and said, "Art, you need Me and I need you." It was the Lord's voice, and I know He called me "Art." I thought, "How wonderful to have this personal Friend talk to me as man to man!" He was saying to me, "I need you"; and I thought, "How in the world can the Lord need *me?*"

Then out of the depths of my need I cried, "Lord, You've got to help me!" I said, "Lord, I'm a coward and a weakling. You know that, for I've proven it to

You during all these years." And I prayed on. "Lord, I want to make the change, but I'm afraid to tell my wife. Please tell her for me and make her willing."

Several weeks later as I sat in the evening service, I was looking to Christ and praying all through the sermon. I do not remember what the subject of the message was, but I do know that at the end of it I found myself at the altar. There I confessed how sinful and helpless I was, and gave myself over to God as completely as I knew how. The heavy burden was lifted, and at last I found the satisfaction I had been seeking for all my life.

Then I started praying for my wife. I did not tell her of the step I had taken, but brought her to the services and prayed that she would become a Christian of her own will independent of any wishes of mine. A few weeks later she did go to the altar and there surrendered her life to Christ.

That night when we went home we said to each other, "Now, at last, we've really got it!" and we wept for joy, a joy that was deeper and more satisfying than anything we had ever experienced before.

Shortly afterward I started to Bible college to prepare for the ministry.

The big question facing us now was whether or not I should continue my work with the various bands and orchestras. I reasoned with myself like this: "Art, you're under a tremendous financial responsibility; you have two children and one is a cripple; you are supporting your deaf brother and his deaf family; you are paying off that ranch; don't you know you've got to keep on making good money?"

I rationalized on still another point as to why I should continue playing. "Art," I said, "don't you know that the people in the world do not hear the gospel? Why don't you stay in your organizations and testify to the boys there?" I felt this to be a strong argument, for I myself had never heard the gospel in all the years of my musical career.

Having proven to myself these two points, I continued with the bands for six months more, studying during the day and playing my trumpet half the night.

The first few months of my Christian life were glorious ones. I had a wonderful time testifying to the fellows in the band, for they, too, were seeking the same thing that I had been seeking. But as our television show was now growing by leaps and bounds, I constantly found less time for witnessing. Often while signing autographs, the Holy Spirit would say, "Give them a testimony," and I would reply, "Not now; I'm busy now, but I will tomorrow." My testimonies became so few that I began to feel myself worse than a sinner; I was claiming to be a Christian and was not letting my light shine.

I prayed, "Lord, what shall I do about this?" I thought of giving up my jobs in the entertainment world, but each time that I would make a move to go, I would get a raise and make more money. Our television show was now reaching half a million.

Two people, a boy and a missionary, brought me to a final decision.

A month after getting one of these raises, I was shopping one day in a Safeway. A man came up to me and said, "You are Art Atwell, aren't you?" I said,

"Yes." He said, "My little boy has been wanting to meet you for a long time. Come here, son." "Oh Art," said the lad as he came over to me, "I see you so often on television, and I want to grow up and be just like you."

That hit me hard. I prayed silently, "Lord, don't let this happen; don't let people envy the life I lead." "Son," I said, "you can stop right now wishing you were in my place. Don't ever again say you want to be like me."

The boy could not believe his own ears. He said, "I've seen you act funny and do handsprings on television." "Yes, I know," I replied, "but God has a different calling for me now. It is to preach the gospel, and I can't do both!" The boy's jaw fell and he gave me an incredible look.

That night I ventured the first step and told my wife that I wanted to give up my worldly employment. To my surprise she said, "Honey, I'm all for you. Don't you dare to back out. Let's do it."

The very next day I listened to a prospective missionary to Communist-controlled China. The missionary whom he was to replace had been put to death. Said he, "The situation is dangerous, and I've got a wife and children, but the Lord called me, and when the Lord calls, I am happy to go." I thought, "Here is a man facing almost certain death, and I am afraid to give up a job!"

That did it. The next day I handed in my resignation.

My resignation was accepted, but there were certain obligations I had to fulfill with the Studio orchestra:

New Year's eve, a record date, and a film to finish. Three weeks later, at nine-thirty, on the very night when I was told that I was reaching a million and a quarter people, I walked out from my last telecast. It was my last engagement in the show world.

I arrived home that Saturday night a little after ten o'clock. As I walked through the doorway, I found my wife reading her Bible. I said, "Honey, I'm a free man!" She said, "I know it!" and we had a season of prayer there, a regular camp-meeting right in our house.

With the exception of the time spent in the service, that was our first Saturday night together in eighteen years.

Since that time I have been busy working for the Lord. My little appointment book is still filled, but not with dates for dances and telecasts and film-making; rather it is filled with names of places where I can tell the people how I finally found that "something" — rather, "Someone"—Whom I had been searching for all my life.

A few days ago, another trumpet player who is still in the world remarked, "You know, I look at you and I've never seen you look so good. You seem to be so happy. I don't know what this being a Christian is all about, but I see peace written in your face. It looks as though the fellows in the world have nothing and you have everything."

I still sometimes say to my wife, "Honey, this time we've really got it!"

We really have found the One we'd both been seeking all our lives.

7   SING US A SONG, BROTHER BENJAMIN

India, the "land of a thousand difficulties," has four hundred million people of whom less than two per cent are Christians. But there are born-again believers. Here is one of them. The story is related by Leoda A. Buckwalter of the Brethren in Christ Mission, Bihar, India.

"Sing us a song, Brother Benjamin," we asked.

The kindly old gentleman with the sweet smile and white hair stood to his feet and moved forward to the front of our crowded little mission church. He was a Santal, one of an aboriginal tribe who live with many others of varying religious beliefs and customs in India. To his right and left sat Christians, all one in Jesus Christ. Could their life stories have been told, they would have spoken of high caste and low, of Hindu, Mohammedan, and, yes, one or two of Christian background. Benjamin too had found the Lord Jesus Christ, and this fact endeared him to the hearts of both missionaries and Indian brethren alike.

So, "Sing us a song in Santali," they said; and Brother Benjamin Mirandy stood in the new little church in Marjora on that warm May day in 1947, and sang. Later he told his story to the group. In faltering Hindi (his native tongue being Santali) he said something like this:

"Brethren and sisters, I know I can not speak very good Hindi, but I want you to know how the Lord Jesus Christ saved me and my family, and I tell this for His glory. I was a 'guru' (teacher) among my people. I worshipped the spirits and knew nothing of the true and living God. I had a son whom I loved dearly. He became exceedingly ill and I was distressed. For his sake I tried everything. My Hindu friends, hearing of my sorrow, told me to forsake the religion of my fathers and turn to their gods. But sacrificing goats and giving to the priests also did no good. My religion had failed, Hinduism had failed. My son was still ill with a dreadful, incurable disease."

The crowded assembly listened attentively. Brother Benjamin continued, "One day, after twelve long years of fruitless trying, I came into a village and saw a group of people listening closely to an Indian village preacher. I pressed my way in, and heard a wonderful and strange story. It seemed that one, a man named Jesus, had miraculously healed a woman who had been ill for twelve years. Twelve years! My son had been ill for twelve years! Maybe this Jesus could do another miracle and heal my son, too. With trembling in my heart I dared to hope. After the meeting I went to the preacher and asked him to take me to Jesus, so that he might also heal my son."

Benjamin's brown face took on a new light, his voice a deep sincerity. "The preacher told me that Jesus could indeed heal my son, but first both I and my whole house must be saved by believing in Him."

Benjamin raised his hand in emphasis, his whole being now radiant with joy.

"And brethren and sisters," he concluded, "both I and my whole house believed on the Lord Jesus and were baptized, and be it known to the glory of the Father that my son was healed! This is the story I tell to my people, for I know it to be true."

8 **A JEW FINDS CHRIST**

Max Cohn is at present a Hebrew evangelist who lives at Winona Lake, Indiana. He wishes to dedicate this story to the two people who led him to the Lord: to Irene Hanley, a Jewess with a heart for her own people, a most able speaker and soul-winner among the Jews; and to Rev. J. C. Lype, a Gentile Christian with a love for Israel who not only helped lead him to Christ but also watched over and helped him when he was still a babe in Christ. For these two he gives special thanks to God.

First of all, I want to tell you that I am a Jew, and if I wanted to deny it, I couldn't, for my countenance betrays me. The Lord Jesus Christ was a Jew; the twelve apostles whom He called out to follow Him were Jews; the writers of the God-inspired words of this Book were Jews. You see, I am happy and proud that I'm a Jew, and I'm not one to deny it.

I have one verse of Scripture that's very near and dear to my heart, because the first time I went to witness for the Lord, I opened my Book, and lo and behold, it fell open to the second book of Timothy, the first chapter. I glanced at it and the first verse that jumped up and hit me was the twelfth verse: "For the which cause I also suffer these things: nevertheless I am not ashamed: for I know whom I have believed, and am persuaded that He is able to keep that which I have committed unto Him against that day." Now isn't that a wonderful verse of Scripture? I have been using it ever since every time I have an opportunity to testify for the Master.

I was born in the city of St. Louis of Jewish orthodox parents and was brought up in the traditions of that kind of home. At an early age we moved into a neighborhood that is, I believe, famous the world over. In those days it was called "Kerry Patch," an Irish neighborhood. It was Irish, and Catholic. We were one of the few Jewish families living in the neighborhood.

This fact was vividly brought home to me the very first day in our new house, when Mother asked me to run an errand for her. As I started out the door I was greeted by a bunch of Gentile boys. They said, "There's the Jew; there's the sheeny; there's the Christ-killer; let's get him." And get me they did. They gave me a good going over. I ran back into the house crying, my clothes torn, my face bleeding, and Mother wanted to know what happened. And I told her. Well, Mother was just like any other mother; she took the wash rag and washed my face, put some clean clothes on me, talked to me like a mother would, and said, "Now son, we live in this neighborhood and you're going to have to get along with those boys. You go and run the errand for Mother."

The seed of hatred was sown in my heart there in that neighborhood. They called me "sheeny" and "a Christ killer." You see I had never killed anybody and I didn't know why they should call me a killer. Then as I grew up and went out into the world, I heard the same thing—only in different words. But no matter where I went, the Jew was always down at the bottom being kicked around.

After some persuading my firm finally got me to go to East St. Louis, and it was there, while standing in the doorway of the store I was managing, that a little lady came by and *handed me a tract.* She said something about the Lord Jesus Christ being the promised Messiah. I looked at the tract and I called her back and said, "Come here; I don't need this; I don't want this." She looked up at me and said, "But you're a Jew, aren't you?" I said, "Sure I'm a Jew," real sarcastic like. You know we Jews are a sarcastic lot when we want to be. And I was very sarcastic to her that day. I told her that I didn't need her tract, that I was all right, and that I was satisfied.

But she proceeded to tell me about my lost and un-done condition, about Christ being the promised Messiah. And I listened to her awhile and she ended her story right quickly and said, "I'll be back to see you." I didn't even invite her back. You know I thank God for people whose hearts are burdened for lost souls. Here was a little lady who was burdened for lost souls. She wasn't taking "No" for an answer. You know, when we deal with people and they say "No" to us, we are prone to say, "Now Lord, I've done my duty. I've spoken to them. I gave them the gospel. Now I'm through with them, Lord." The next day the little lady not only came back herself but she brought her pastor with her. How I thank God for that pastor! He walked up to me, shook hands with me, talked to me a while, and then put his arm around me and said, looking me squarely in the eye, "Max, you know, I love you."

Well, I never did have anybody to tell me that he loved me. I thought everybody hated the Jew. I didn't think anybody had any time for the Jews. It's the first time in my life I ever had anybody put his arm around me and tell me that he loved me. And I looked right back at him and said, "Why do you love me? Why do you say that you love me?" He said, "I love you because Christ loves you, because I have the love of Christ in my heart. And that love is for you and for all humanity." And he went on to tell me about it. You know, he all but melted me that afternoon. Before he left he gave me an invitation to his church.

After repeated invitations, I finally went. I did what most people do when they go to church—I sat in the back row. I sat back there so I could get out quickly, and that's what I did. The second time I went I was met at the door and was escorted down to about the third row. That night (I don't know how many of you have ever had this experience) that preacher preached only to me. I sat there and I said to myself, "I'm glad I learned how to duck punches because this preacher is surely throwing plenty of them at me tonight." And I just sat there and moved from one place to the other, dodging everything that he threw at me. It seemed to me that I was the only one in the congregation that night. And when it was all over I tried to get out, but they had me down in the third row and I couldn't get out.

After the service that preacher walked over to me and put his arm around me and said, "You know, I'd like for you to come with me to my house." I couldn't understand why this man liked me so well, and I went over to his house. And there for the first time in my life the plan of salvation was made plain. That man poured his heart out from the time we left the church until one o'clock in the morning. And when he finished he said, "Well, Max, what are you thinking?"

You know what a smart aleck would say, don't you? I was a smart aleck. I was a Jew. I was brought up in Judaism. He wasn't going to sell me Christianity. I wanted no part in it. Christ was not the Messiah to me. He was just an impostor. He was an illegitimate child, as far as I was concerned. I was still waiting for the Messiah to come. I turned around to the preacher and I said, "Preacher, that's a good sales talk, but you can't sell it to me." I have gone back many times since to ask that preacher to forgive me.

I went home that night. I couldn't sleep. You see, I was still in sin. I smoked one cigarette after another, trying to get some sleep, but there was no sleep in me. The next day as I was standing in the doorway of that store, the preacher passed by. He said, "Hello there, Max, how are you feeling this morning?" I said, "I don't feel so good this morning." He said, "What's the matter?" I said, "I didn't sleep last night. I just didn't rest." He said, "Praise the Lord." I said, "What are you praising the Lord for, preacher?" He said, "I prayed that you wouldn't sleep and that you wouldn't rest until you have turned it all over to Christ." I said, "Don't you pray for me like that any more, preacher." (But I've done it many a time since, myself — many a time!)

I was getting to the place now where I knew that I ought to be a Christian. But I had a lot of sin in my life. I smoked, I cussed, I drank, I danced, I gambled. I said to the missionary, "Now, look; I've got that much sense to know that in order to be a Christian I've got to

49

give up these things, but *I can't do it.*" Her reply was in just a few words, "Leave it to God." That remark struck home to my heart, and the more I thought about it, the more it convicted me. I was fighting conviction for all I was worth. After all, wasn't I a Jew and one of God's chosen people? I didn't need any Christianity. No matter what happened, I was still God's child. That was what I tried to think.

One day I got an invitation to an Easter sunrise service. There I heard the story of Christ's death, His burial, and His resurrection. That morning I was so convicted when I left that mount that I just couldn't stand still for a second. When we got to the missionary's home for breakfast, I couldn't eat. When we started for church, she said to me, "Why don't you turn it all over to God this morning, Max?" I never answered her. When I got to the church, I went over to the men's class in the corner. And somebody evidently had put a pin cushion there, because I couldn't sit there two seconds. Then I spied the preacher over in the corner getting ready to make his rounds of the Sunday School. I almost ran to him and said, "Preacher, I wonder if you wouldn't pray with me this morning. I feel in need of something." He smiled and put his arm around me. He knew what was up and walked me down to his study. And there on my knees, I was not only letting tears run down my cheeks, but I was crying out loud. I was so convicted. The preacher got down on his knees and cried out to God on my behalf, and when he finished, he said, "Now you talk to God in your own way."

That morning, that Easter morning twelve years ago, I cried out to God to forgive me, a sinner. I told God

I believed in His only begotten Son, that I believed He was the promised Messiah, that I believed He came into the world and went to Calvary's cross, that I believed His blood would wash my sins white as snow, pure as wool. And, oh, I tell you, beloved, that morning when the whole world seemed to be weighing me down, dragging me into the very bowels of the earth, that burden was lifted and my soul was flooded with joy and a song was put into my mouth.

Now the first thing you want to do after you are saved is to go out and tell the world about it. And the first place you want to go is home. That is what I wanted to do. I wanted to go home. I wanted to tell my people. I wanted to tell them that I had found the Messiah. I wanted to tell them that Christ is alive, that He is real, that we didn't have to wait for Him. So I went over to St. Louis to see my Dad.

"Oh, Dad," I said, "I want to tell you about the Messiah. I met Him face to face and my sins are all forgiven. He lives. You don't have to wait for him." He looked at me a moment, and said, "Are you well? Do you feel all right?" I said, "No, I'm not joking with you, Dad. I'm serious. I'm dead serious about this. You know, I'm not a child. You know that I'm a grown man. I don't have to talk bedtime stories to you. I'm in dead earnest about this." He said, "I'm afraid you are going insane. I'm afraid you belong in an insane asylum." Then as I continued pressing my message to him he ordered me out of his house. As I was leaving I told him I would be praying for him.

Years went by and never once could I put my foot into their home. If I wanted to see them I had to drive by in my automobile and catch a glimpse of Mother as she sat out on the porch or of Dad as he was coming from work. That's the way I got to see them.

Then one day I got a phone call. They told me Mother was sick over in such and such a hospital. When I got there I found that my mother was paralyzed. I went out into the corridor of that hospital and prayed to God that He might let Mother live so that she could be saved before she went out into eternity. God heard my prayer. Yes, she was a paralytic, but God raised her up. Now, how was I going to give her the gospel? I was worried about that. But you know God takes care of everything. He works in mysterious ways His wonders to perform.

Then another incident happened in my life. My Dad took sick. I got a call telling me that he was dying. He had just about an hour or so to live, they told me. I rushed to the hospital fast. When I got there I met my sisters and my brothers-in-law and several friends. I said, "Well, what's the verdict?" They told me that Dad had a minor operation which turned into a major one and that he had lost so much blood that there was no hope for him. I said, "Have they tried everything?" They said, "Yes." "Where is the doctor?" I asked. "He's not here, but he's coming," they said. When the doctor came I was the first one to greet him. I said, "Doctor, have we done everything that we can for Dad?" And I asked for a blood transfusion. The doctor said about six of us should go upstairs and be typed. We went up. Of the bunch, I was the only one who had the same type as Dad.

I'll never forget that experience as long as I live. As I went into that room and lay there on that table and they put the needle into my arm and started to draw the blood from my veins, I caught a glimpse of the Lord as He hung on the tree on Calvary and was pouring out His blood that I might have life and have it eternally. I cried out to God that the blood that was being drawn from my veins might save my dad, that he might hear the gospel and that he too might turn from his wicked ways and seek God's face. I prayed that he too might come to the place where he would cry out, "Oh, God, forgive me, a sinner."

As soon as they drew that needle from my arm, they thrust a glass of orange juice into my hand. I started to get down from that table. They tried to hold me, but I said, "I'm going down stairs." They said, "No, you can't. You must stay up here and rest a while." I said, "I can't rest here," and I ran down the steps. When I got down there, they were already giving Dad that transfusion. The doctor stood in the door and he was smiling. He said, "A miracle has happened." I told him that God was still performing miracles. I told him that the God I had put my trust and faith in performed a miracle when He saved me, and I knew that when I cried out to God on that table that He would answer my prayer. I knew it.

When Dad returned home I was permitted to go in and out of my father's home, and I had the opportunity of opening God's Word to him. Today he is living with me in *my* home; and although he has not yet yielded to Christ, his heart is softening, and I am still praying and I still have faith in God that I'll see the day, even though he is past seventy, when he will cry out to God.

Let me tell you one more incident about Mother. I got a call. You see, I lived on the other side of the river, and every time they wanted to contact me they had to telephone. So they called me and told me to come over, saying that it was the last for Mother. She had suffered another paralytic stroke. This time she was completely paralyzed. When I got there I looked at Mother. I pulled on her arm, her wrist. I said, "Mother, Mother, do you know me?" Not an answer. I tugged at her a little bit more, and I said, "Mother, do you know me?" Not an answer. I moved her lips. Her tongue was very thick. I knew she couldn't talk to me. I looked into her eyes, and her eyes were open, and I sensed a situation. I reached out with my hand over her eyes, and I knew that she was blind. I prayed to God, "Oh, God, give her just one minute, sixty seconds, that I might ask her *the question*, that I might tell her about Jesus and say that He is able to save even now. You see, it was *my* mother. She had gone into the valley of death to bring me into the world. She had suffered many a heartache because of me. I had put many a grey hair in her head because I was a disobedient boy. She was my mother and I loved her with all my heart. I realized that she was going out into eternity without God, without Christ, and I was crying out to God to give her just sixty seconds that she might hear me in that one moment. As I tugged on her, I kept saying, "Mother, won't you put your trust and faith in the Lord?" I kept tugging at her arm and I kept speaking to God, asking Him to give her just that sixty seconds, that one minute.

Ah, we have a wonderful God, One who is able. How I praise God; how I thank God! Just in that moment when I was crying out to God, Mother's mouth broke out in a smile. As I tugged at her arm begging her to put her trust and faith in the Lord, her eyes moved and her head moved. She seemed to know where I was standing. As she turned her head and looked at me, I said, "Mother, won't you put your trust and faith in the Lord?" and as she smiled she *nodded her head.* Just a little while later she went out into eternity, but I am satisfied in my heart today that I am going to meet Mother some day.

Oh, I wouldn't exchange today the joy of this wonderful salvation for all the money that you could give me. There are those who know that I will never make in the religious world the money I made in the business world, but money doesn't bother me today. I wouldn't go back for all the money in the world. There is never such joy as there is in going about witnessing for the Lord Jesus Christ. But, oh, beloved, how lax we have been in witnessing for the Master! I praise God that even in the late years of my life He has called me. He has given me the privilege of going into the highways and byways to tell the most wonderful story in all the world.

* * *

9 **THE PREACHER'S KID**

Phil Kerr is a versatile musical evangelist: pianist, author, composer, and musical authority. More than twelve hundred songs have come from his pen. His writings appear regularly in national periodicals. He is the author of a musical history, now in its third edition, which is a standard textbook in colleges and seminaries.

A songbook containing many of his better-known compositions is now in its fifteenth edition, and includes such national favorites as "In Love with the Lover of My Soul" and "Over in Glory." He has made more than seventy coast-to-coast concert tours, presenting gospel song concerts in every state. He is said to have one of the largest libraries of books pertaining to hymnology.

One who has attended his now famous Monday night "Musical" in Pasadena does not easily forget the warmth, the informality, and the spiritual blessing of these gospel music programs.

Phil Kerr is a passionate soul-winner. He likes nothing better than to kidnap Hollywood "stars" for Christ (as, for instance, Marylin Hall and Arnie Hartman), leading them to a penitential confession of sin and acceptance of Christ as Savior, and then to see them dedicate themselves and their talents to the service of Christ. And no one can ever compute the number of souls won by the songs that flow out from his heart and pen. God bless his ministry in melody.

Although my initials, "P. K.," proclaim that I am a "Preacher's Kid," I nevertheless needed to be born again. Yes, even preachers' kids need to be born again. Emphatically so!

Dad and Mother were missionaries, the old-fashioned kind who chose the hardest places and usually worked without the financial support of a missionary board.

Mother's dad was a wealthy atheist in Ohio. When she became a Christian, in her teens, he practically disowned her. She went to New York City and worked her way through a missionary training school, sitting at the feet of Dr. A. B. Simpson, the great missionary statesman. After working for a period in the slums of New York's Bowery district, she journeyed to the pioneer mining towns in the Colorado mountains—and it was there that she met my father.

Dad had been raised on the prairies of Western Saskatchewan, and never went to school until he was grown. While still in his youth he had been born again and felt the call to preach. At the age of twenty-one he went to Eastern Canada, acquired an education and seminary training, and became a preacher. Later, he too felt the missionary urge to go to the Colorado mining towns, and it was there that he met my mother—or did I already say that?

Dad worked with his hands as a miner in Colorado and Arizona, as a blacksmith in Mexico, as a longshoreman in San Pedro. He'd work all day, and then preach half the night—or so it seemed to me! We'd have long "family prayers," and long Bible studies, and long street meetings, and long gospel services in the mission (every night in the year), and long bedtime prayers. Oh yes, and long "altar services" every night at the close of the meeting.

As I look back on it now, I am extremely thankful for such a solid spiritual foundation. Christ was an important member of our family circle. Every day I read the motto on the wall by the kitchen table: "Christ is the Head of this house, the Unseen Guest at every meal, the Silent Listener to every conversation." We brought Him all our troubles, we told Him all our joys and sorrows, and we depended upon Him for our daily bread.

One night, after supper, we had our regular period of family prayers. As we arose from our knees I said to mother, "Mamma, I asked Jesus to save me, and I believe He did." I was only six years of age, but I had the positive assurance that I had been born again.

I wish however I could report that I followed the Lord implicitly from that time forward. I'm sorry to insert the fact that such was not the case. I felt the Lord's hand upon my life, and I knew definitely that He had plans for me; but I fiercely resented the poverty and the insecurity of a missionary life. I longed for material security and for the good things of life that other people had. I therefore started out to get those things.

But thank God, there came a time when Christ's call became so insistent that I could no longer resist. I discovered that getting the hands full, and the pockets full, and the bank accounts full, did not always get the heart full.

I'll never forget the night when I made complete surrender to the will of God for my life. I gave up my secular job and my worldly ambitions, and since then have been trying to let the Lord's complete will be wrought in my life. The result has been a constant joy and a deep-seated peace which can not be found outside of the will of God.

Yes, thank God, I'm a new creature in Christ Jesus. I have been born again, and I am going to live forever with Him who "saved me by His grace."

MY ACCORDION FOR CHRIST

Recognized as a top accordionist, Arnie Hartman discontinued his professional career when, in October, 1949, he confessed Christ as his Savior. His check for the last week that he played in the entertainment world was sixteen hundred dollars.

Arnie still plays his accordion. In fact, he feels that he should play even better than before, now that he is doing it for the glory of the Lord and not for the world. Only recently he achieved a complicated feat which no other living accordionist can perform.

And with his playing of hymns and gospel songs goes an effervescent testimony—effervescent because he evidences such genuine and running-over joy in his new-found relationship to God.

As far as the professional world goes, I have had a full life. I want to tell you about some of these experiences, and I relate them not from an egotistic standpoint, but that they may serve only as an understandable background to *the* great climaxing experience, my conversion. I do it all for the glory of my Lord and Savior Jesus Christ.

I was a normal kid; had to take my bath on Saturday night and go to Sunday School on Sunday morning. When I was twelve years of age, I was hit by a car which fractured my skull and ripped me open inside. Through the coaxing and the threats of my mother, I took my spinach and codliver oil, and I slowly recovered my health. One of the rewards for my bravery and faithfulness was to be a bicycle.

The day came when we started down town for the bicycle. On the way we passed a music store. In the window of that store was a piano accordion. I had never before been so close to one, and it intrigued me. Mother weakened, and in no time we were inside, examining it. From my experience on our piano at home I was able to play a tune on it.

Soon the clerk was saying, "Arnie, you take this accordion home and play it for ten days, and if you play well when you come back, you can go on the radio and on kiddie reviews, and you can pay for the accordion yourself."

"How much does the instrument cost?" my mother asked.

The man said, "Six hundred dollars."

My mother almost fell over. That was a whole lot more than the thirty-five dollars we had expected to pay for the bicycle. We finally settled for a cheaper instrument.

And that is how I got started on the accordion.

I took it home, and when I returned ten days later I could play anything I had ever heard, whistled, or hummed. I just seemed to fall into that thing and it came natural to me.

I soon got into a kiddies' review, and that was the beginning of show business for me. From then on, it just seemed that with everything I did, everywhere I turned, more offers kept coming in all the time.

Then we moved to the West Coast and my health pepped up. I found there still more work; jobs were coming in faster and the money was getting bigger all the time.

The first thing I knew I was stuck in the business. I got my schooling the hard way — through Hollywood professional schools—just so I could stay in the show business.

I was playing back and forth across the country. Then I was signed up for a fifty-two-week show, and that gave me the taste of a regular big circuit. And then came the invitations from abroad: Hawaiian Islands, Australia, Calcutta, Bombay — the whole southwestern hemisphere.

While over there I got into everything that a fellow can get into. I was alone. I was making big money; in fact, new foreign artists usually received triple their worth. I was being paid in English pounds, and in those days they were big five-dollar pounds.

I next headed for Central and South America. For five years I played the main cities, and finally ended up in Mexico City.

One day in Mexico City I received a letter from my dad. The letter said, "Arnie, I don't think your mother is feeling her best and if you can make tracks home you'd better do it." I had never received a letter like that. I read some things between the lines and I told the boys I was quitting. Immediately I sent telegrams, one to New York and one to Chicago, accepting two professional engagements, the ones I played just before my conversion three years ago. I played these engagements—the Oriental Theatre in Chicago and the Flamingo Hotel in Las Vegas—on the way to my home in Hollywood.

When I arrived home I found my suspicions confirmed. I never saw my mother looking so bad. For many years I hadn't thought of God, but now I did and, sinner as I was, I began to pray for her right then and there. I don't know if He heard my prayer, or someone else's, but do you know that my mother today is as well as she has ever been in her life. For that I really have to be thankful.

I now told my representatives to start booking me here in my own country. I had had enough of experience in foreign lands; and then too, I wanted to be closer home.

Several days after I was home the telephone rang. The voice on the other end said, "I don't think you know me, Arnie, but my name is Phil Kerr. You may have heard of me through a mutual friend, Ray Odegard." Immediately I knew whom he meant. Ray is pianist for Sol Hopi, the world's best player on the Hawaiian electric guitar. My mother had told Ray that I was coming home, and Ray had told Phil. How much more goes with that story I'm not exactly sure, but I think there is more than I know, because things could not have happened the way they did without some real conscientious praying. Now, as I look back on it, I am more convinced than ever that that was the case.

Phil Kerr said, "Arnie, I put on a program here every Monday night (his famous *Musicals*). I'd like you to come over and take a look and see what you think of it and maybe give us a classical number." Phil Kerr was asking *me*, who had just come from one of the country's swankiest resorts where gambling goes on twenty-four hours a day, to come and play on this religious program! I was feeling pretty nervous and I didn't want to be bothered, so I said, "Maybe some other day. I just got home and want to rest." I hung up and thought I'd be gone in just a few more days, and it wouldn't make much difference.

But it wasn't as easy as all that. Several days later this Phil Kerr phoned again. "Say, Arnie," he said, "how about having a sandwich and a cup of coffee together?" I thought, "What is he calling me for? I've never met him; after all, he's no pal of mine!"

Well, anyway, I went over and met Phil Kerr. Here was a man who stole my curiosity right off the bat. His personality electrified me. You who know Phil Kerr know what I mean. He has a magnetic something about him that just makes you like him. Of course I know now what it is; it is the life of Christ in the man; that is exactly what gives him his tremendous personality.

I was invited to their home one day for dinner — Phil says *supper*—and after the meal, together with a few other guests, we sat around the room talking and playing the piano. I had my little "Steinway" there, and I played a few classical numbers. Listen, I was having the best time there that evening that I ever had in my life, and I was thinking to myself, "And all of this for nothing!" You see, I had become so accustomed to having to lay the dough on the line for all the fun that I had ever had in life; I used to have to plunk down the money. Now here this night I was having one of the finest, and it was costing me nothing, and I just couldn't get over that.

And as I sat reflecting thus in his home that night, Phil Kerr said to me, "Arnie, we have a custom here where each evening we read a bit of Scripture and then drop to our knees and kinda thank God for what He's done in our lives." He was looking right over at me all the time. There were others there; I don't know why he didn't look at them, too; it made me feel funny. I said, "Well, sure, I don't care; go ahead."

And then I started to get the turning of the heart. If any of you know Phil, you know how he explains things in a sort of down-to-earth way, with no big words, in just the simplest way. I tell you, the fellow just crawls right inside of you. Anyway, he did me, and he started to chew on my heart. I don't remember what verse it was he was discussing, but I do know that it started me to thinking just how small I really was and how useless in the kind of work I was in. Phil's discussion was the entering wedge.

Then they all went down on their knees. I was the last one sitting up. I looked around and felt it was stupid to sit there like that, so I got down too.

And that's when the thing really happened. My heart really started to break. Never in my life had I felt like I did there that evening. I saw myself as I really was, just an old reprobate, an old sinner, lost all these years, sick and tired of the world, sick and tired of all the sham. And I knew right then and there, friends, that I needed God in my life; otherwise I didn't know where I would end up. So I started to pray, and believe me now, I *prayed!* I was so engrossed in just getting right with God that that was all I cared about. If I could just get right with God! I was really praying. Towards the end I could hear myself praying. But then I didn't care who heard me, for I had already decided to pray up to the victory point.

Phil told me later how I had surprised the whole group. "Why, Arnie," he said, "we were all through praying and half up off our knees, when, lo and behold, you started to pray. We hadn't expected that. So we all got back down on our knees again."

Now I want to tell you something, friends. Do you know why I know that Christ really lives? I'll tell you why. Because on my knees that night in Phil Kerr's home, I prayed, "O God, forgive me for the awful life I've been living and give me just one more chance." And God heard that prayer and He answered it, and instead of that terrible weight of sin, He gave me great joy. Some of the others were shouting, "Glory, praise the Lord!" and Phil got a little excited, but I didn't care; for the battle was over.

For five days after that night, such a terrific happiness, such a c-l-e-a-n happiness and joy came into my heart, it seemed to me that the Lord and I were all alone. I don't remember much about anything else. It felt as though I had a hold of one of God's circuits with plenty of power in it.

Now let me tell you something that is truly marvelous. During those five days, I forgot that I was a smoker of cigarettes. I said to myself, "Something's different! What is it?" And all of a sudden it dawned on me that I used to be a smoker of cigarettes. Where was the lighter? Where was the little stove with the gasoline? And the cigarettes themselves? And it just dawned on me that they were g-o-n-e !

To show just how marvelous a deliverance this really was, let me tell you that I had been smoking four packs of cigarettes a day.

And I want to tell you something else: Since that evening I've never even thought of a drop of liquor,

n-e-v-e-r ! That's as far away from me as though I had
never tasted it. As a result, about three weeks after I
was saved, I had to go and buy new clothes, for I was
splitting at the seams. So you see I became a new man
physically as well as spiritually.

Well, praise the Lord, that night changed my whole
life!

Believe me, friends, I consider it a marvel that God
had enough grace to save me, for I was in pretty bad
shape. I was a pretty tough sinner. And believe me
again, if the Lord can save me, He can save *anybody*.

I'm in the work now for the Lord, and that is exactly
where I intend to stay for the rest of my life.

* * *

11   **. . . BUT SAINT JOHN WASN'T A SISSY**

*"From Times Square, New York, we bring you the
Word of Life . . . on the air!" When these words were
first uttered on the evening of October 25, 1941, not
even Jack Wyrtzen was aware that this split-second
Gospel broadcast was to mark the beginning of the
thousands of Saturday night youth rallies that are being
held over the world today. Although Wyrtzen's voice
has become familiar to millions in his near decade of
broadcasting, many do not know the story of his own
conversion.*

*Here Wyrtzen describes the experience in his own
words, his personal testimony as given in the Madison
Square Garden Rally, September 29, 1945. From "God
Hath Chosen" by Forrest Forbes, Zondervan Publishing
House.*

Before I was saved, in the evenings I was leading a dance orchestra and playing for fraternity clubs and sorority dances. In the daytime I was working in the insurance business. But along with all this, I joined up with the 101st Cavalry Band in Brooklyn, and there I played my trombone one night a week on horseback in the United States Cavalry Band.

With a busy life like this I'll tell you that I didn't find very much time for God and the Bible—until one night a young fellow by the name of George, who was then my buddy in the United States Army Band, came to me and handed me a Gospel of Saint John. I looked at him and asked him what the idea was, for he was the last one I'd ever expect to see with a Bible under his arm. Then he told me how he had taken the Lord Jesus as his personal Savior and had been wonderfully saved. I told him that I wasn't the least bit interested, and I tried to hand the Gospel of John back. But he insisted that I at least take it home with me.

Well, I finally took the Gospel of John to be polite, and I put it into my pocket. Then later, on my way home, while I was standing at the railroad station with my trombone under my arm, I put my hand into my pocket and there I found the Gospel of Saint John. I took it out and read, "Gospel of Saint John." I thought it would have been bad enough if it had said "Gospel of John," but "Gospel of *Saint* John," mind you—*Saint* John! Somehow that *Saint* business seemed to burn me up. I thought, *Boy what a sissy, what a holy Joe I'd be, carrying around a Gospel of "Saint" John.* So I took the Gospel of John and I tore it to pieces and threw it off the railroad station platform.

Friend, that's what I thought of God's Word a few years back. Little did I realize that night, as I stood there brazenly tearing God's Word to pieces, that it would only be a few months later when this very Book, God's Word, would tear me to pieces and I'd see myself as a sinner, lost and needing the Savior that the Bible tells of.

Well, that was in January, one cold winter's night, when I tore up the Gospel of John. The following Monday night at the band rehearsal I met George again and the first question he asked me was, "Jack, how are you getting along with the Gospel of John I gave you last week?" I said, "Gospel of John? What Gospel? Oh," I said, "you mean that little red book." He said, "Yes, have you read it?" I said, "Read it? Why, George, I threw it away before I got home." He said, "Did you? Well, here's another one." "Oh," I said, "now look here, George, let's not go into that again." Week after week George kept handing me tracts and Gospels, and the more he handed me the more I threw away.

Six months went by and we went off to army camp together. I thought, surely this fellow George will forget all about his old religion in this man's army with all the drinking, gambling, cursing, filth, and debauchery. I knew that the summer before, George had committed every sin right down the line that a soldier could commit.

The first day that we were away there at army camp, I heard several of the fellows using the name of the Lord in vain, dragging it down into the gutter. I saw George speak to one of them, and he said, "Listen, fellow, the Name you're dragging down is the Name that's taking me up to heaven." That hit me! Then, too, I knew that a Christian would read his Bible and get down on his knees to pray before going to bed. And I thought, surely George will never read his Bible and pray with those fellows around.

Taps sounded, lights went out, and George hadn't read his Bible or prayed. And we all lay there on our cots thinking, He's scared to do it. But wait a minute! George reached down into his barracks bag and grabbed hold of his Bible and flashlight and there he sat on the edge of his cot! I can see him yet. He read for a while and then got down on his knees for prayer. We could curse at him, throw shoes or anything else, but he stayed there until he was through. He was a man!

And after watching this fellow for two full weeks, twenty-four hours a day, there in that army camp, and noting the marvelous change in his life, I decided he had something that I didn't have, and whatever he had, I wanted.

That summer after we came back from the army camp I got hold of a Gospel of John. I started to read it through. The following fall the band got together again and my buddy, George, invited me to a little meeting over in Brooklyn where the gospel would be preached. One after another got to his feet and told what Christ meant to him.

This was all new to me, for outside of George's testimony I'd never heard anything like it before. But that night, in His grace, God brought me under deep conviction. I got mad. I didn't like the way the preacher talked about sin, righteousness, and the judgment to come. He spoke about a real heaven and a real hell, and about the second coming of the Lord Jesus Christ. He spoke to us straight from the shoulder and told us that the only hope of heaven was in the new birth.

I didn't like it. I left the meeting mad, but that night at home, in the blackness of my room as I lay on my bed, it seemed as though all the blackness of eternity loomed up before me, and I realized for the first time in my life that I, too, was a sinner, but that Jesus Christ, God's Son, died and shed His blood on the Cross of Calvary for me. Somehow I slipped out of bed; I got down on my knees and admitted to God above that my life had been stained, marred, and blackened with sin. Then I asked Him right there and then to save me for Jesus' sake.

I don't remember just how or what I prayed that night, but I know that I passed from death unto life, from the power of Satan unto God. My eyes were opened and forgiveness of sins became my portion. That night Jesus Christ became real to me; and what He did for me, beloved, He can and will do for you if you'll only "behold the Lamb of God, which taketh away the sin of the world."

* * *

12   FOUR DOLLARS AND VICTORY

"Excuse me, but my emotions get away with me when I think of those four dollars," Benjamin Engstrom, better known as "Curley," apologized as, wiping tears, he related the following details across a table in the lounge of the Old Pacific Garden Mission.

CONVERSION STORIES

Since "Curley's" new birth, he has been offered a position as electrician at Wheaton College; but because of his appreciation for the Mission where he learned the love of his Savior, and for the Mission's superintendent, Harry Saulnier, he persistently refuses to leave the work at 626 South State. It is his consuming desire to help others find the deliverance he himself has found.

For twenty-nine and one-half years I was general electrical foreman in the largest steel mill in the world, having charge of thirteen all-electric rolling mills, and supervising never less than two hundred men.

Sounds boastful, doesn't it?

I do not intend it as such; I say it because I want to show how long a slide downward from that responsible position I had taken when I finally landed on Chicago's "Skidrow."

The Gary, Indiana, Steel Mill did not fire me when I first started drinking. They tolerated me, apologized for me, and even recommended a complete Keeley Cure treatment in hopes of rehabilitating me and getting me to leave the stuff alone.

They were successful for a while. But eventually I started down the incline and, because of my increasing irresponsibility, they were forced, reluctantly, to let me go.

Then *I* let go, and the succeeding period of my life can be designated as one long drunk. In a semi-stupor and with dulled sensibilities I floated from bar to bar, from cheap vaudeville show to sports gambling joint, until I cared little what would happen next.

Out of a family of two brothers and nine sisters, I thus became the "black sheep." They were ashamed of me. My own sons, whom I had placed in responsible positions in the steel mill before my exit, became embarrassed whenever my name was mentioned.

One day in March, 1945, I happened past a noonday street meeting. I overheard something being said about electricity and I stopped to listen.

I was "hooked!" The Holy Spirit stopped me in my tracks, and my interest was transferred from the subject of electricity to the spiritual lesson the speaker was illustrating.

Later, in response to their invitation I went to the Pacific Garden Mission Gospel Hall and there, praise God! something definitely and unquestionably happened inside of me. I was gloriously saved.

Although I had eaten but little food for weeks, and my stomach was wrenched and rebellious, I slept soundly all night in the bed the Mission provided. That I slept all night was itself a miracle.

But the miracle the next morning was greater still: *I was able to put my hand into my pocket.* That may not mean much to you who read this, but let me tell you that the night before I had not been able to raise a tin cup to my mouth even by using both hands.

Add to this a third miracle: When I put my hand into my pocket, *I found there four one-dollar bills* which I didn't know I had.

Now mark this. Here's the miracle of all miracles: After I was dressed, I left my hotel room and went down the street, past the old saloons I had visited daily, **to the Mission,** *and I had four dollars in my hand!*

Ask any alcoholic if passing a favorite saloon with four dollars in hand is possible, especially after a night of abstinence, and he will say it is humanly not possible. Here is the proof of the pudding that something had really happened in the heart of this old bum the night before at the Pacific Garden Mission altar! No one can ever know what a sense of joy and triumph the feel of those four one-dollar bills meant when I reached the Mission that memorable morning.

I have often been asked if the smell of liquor has not become obnoxious to me. In all honesty I must say that it has not. I could very easily take a drink and I would have a taste for it.

But I am glad that the same Power that kept me from spending those four dollars that first morning after my conversion has likewise been keeping me steady ever since. I have not tasted one drop of liquor since that time. "Thanks be to God who giveth us the victory through our Lord Jesus Christ."

Furthermore, I have, through God, regained the confidence of my family and of my professional associates. One of my sons said to me the other day, "Dad, we were proud of you when you held the high position in the steel mill, but we are more proud of you now because of the work you are doing at the mission."

One of the head men of the steel mill passed the Mission recently and saw me washing windows. He stopped and said, "Curley, what are you doing here?" He didn't know that Pacific Garden Mission is my spiritual birthplace, that it is now my "home," and that, instead of maintaining contacts on the electric apparatus of the big steel rolling mills, I intend to devote the rest of my life to putting lost souls on "Skid-row" in contact with a Supremely Dynamic Power that can raise them up out of their vomit and defeat, even as I have been lifted up.

* * *

13   **AN UNSPECTACULAR NEW BIRTH**

Dr. J. A. Huffman, president of Winona Lake School of Theology and author of a score of books on the Bible, Theology, and Archeology, has made repeated visits to the Holy Land. A minister of the United Missionary Church, Dr. Huffman is also critical editor of the Higley Sunday School Lesson Commentaries.

The story of my conversion is of such a nature that those who are looking for the spectacular only would not give it space in such a volume as this.

In using the term, "new birth," to express the experience which came into my life at the age of eleven years, I give it the meaning that Jesus did in His nighttime conversation with Nicodemus: "That which is born of the Spirit is spirit." The new birth is not the beginning of life itself, but is instead the beginning of a *quality* of life which is eternal and spiritual; it is the eternal right relation between God and man, wrought through the Holy Spirit. Were the new birth merely the beginning of life, then it might be argued that without it there is no immortality. Again, I can not concur with the pressing of analogies between the physical birth and the spiritual birth too far, for in the physical birth the one born has had no choice and is inescapably and unceasingly a son, while in the spiritual birth one is born as the result of the choice of a free moral agent.

The very unspectacular aspect of my new birth constitutes its spectacular feature. I was saved from drunkenness, profanity, gambling, adultery, card playing, carousing, dancing, and wicked things too numerous to mention, for I had engaged in none of them; God saved me from them by keeping me out of them. Herein lies the marvel! Without minimizing the glorious conversion experiences of "big sinners," I nevertheless hold that by all correct logic, to be saved *from* sins is a greater miracle than to be saved *out of* sins, even though a less spectacular miracle.

I do not mean to give the impression that I was not badly in need of the new birth. I, indeed, felt myself a big sinner on that night before Christmas, in my eleventh year. The seeking, the repentance, and the faith which I exercised, even though that of a child, were very real, and always in speaking of my initial Christian experience I point back to that time and place.

The new birth, however, was not an end, not "the one big thing," but the small beginning of a spiritual life which, funnel-like, opened up into tremendously big and richer comprehensions of divine truth.

My conversion came about in this way:

I was attending a series of revival meetings held in an old school house in Northern Indiana, the grade school of which I was a pupil. One evening when the altar call was being given, the evangelist came back through the audience and, laying his hand on my shoulder, asked me if I did not want to become a Christian. I could not truthfully deny, and so said, "Yes." He then asked me if I did not want to be saved *now,* and again I confessed. His next question brought results; he asked me if I would not come with him for prayer. I followed, and knelt at the long bench on which I had that very day made my school recitations. That old recitation bench had suddenly become my "mourner's bench," my altar. From that altar of prayer I went to my home a Christian lad, to follow out all the meanings of my new-found life as I would come to them.

Not to my praise, but to the glory of God, I can say that from that day to this I have never known backsliding. I am not a "self-made man," but a "grace-made man!" There have been many blunders and some failures, but throughout my life I have constantly sought to right every wrong immediately upon its discovery, and to walk in the light as it has come to me.

* * *

14 SOMETIMES GOD CALLS LOUDLY

L. E. Showalter is a locomotive engineer on the Burlington Railroad. He lives in Houston, Texas.

In the earlier part of my life I never felt a need of being saved. I was a "good, respectable, moral man." Everyone knew that I neither drank nor smoked. There wasn't even any need for me to go to church.

It took three providences of God to awaken me — this "good, respectable, moral man"—to the fact that I was a sinner who needed saving.

The first of these calls was mild. My wife, who for a number of years had been attending the Christian Science church, broke with that doctrine and was happily saved through simple faith in Christ. She urged me to join with her in this new-found joy and faith. I did sometimes go with her to church, but persistently refused in my heart to admit that I needed a Savior.

The second call was rough. One night the headlight on my locomotive disclosed a prostrate body on the adjacent track. Stopping my train, I found that the torn and mangled form was that of my close friend, a fellow-trainman, who had fallen under the wheels of his own train a few minutes before. I found myself asking seriously, "What if it had been I?"

The third call of God was thunder in my ears. One week later my engine ran into an open switch, swerved crosswise, and turned over onto its side. Amidst escaping steam, I crawled out of my cab, unscathed. But during the brief moments that it took for my engine to come to rest on its side, I had a kaleidoscopic view of every act and thought of my past life, and I knew beyond the shadow of a doubt that it was God speaking and that I needed a Savior.

"I'm ready to give up," were the words that I said both to my wife and to the Lord that evening when I walked into the kitchen. God took me at my word and forgave my sins. A few days later I confessed Christ publicly as my Lord and Savior.

* * *

15   **I FORGOT GOD**

By Louis Zamparini, as related to the compiler of this book in private interview.

To turn down an offer of fifty thousand dollars a year for a period of seven years under the conditions here stated, is certainly an acid test of one's loyalty to his Lord and Savior.

It would be hard to find a life more filled with miracle than mine. In fact, even before I had reached my teens, people were remarking that I had a charmed life, and dubbed me "Luckie Louie." When my life is viewed from the purely human angle, the word that springs most naturally to the tongue is "Incredible!" Without taking God into the picture, the successes, the coincidents, the rescues, and the so-called "good luck" remain mysteries which will not let themselves be explained by nature or science. There just can not be any other answer than that the God who notices the fall of every sparrow kept His protecting hand over me when time and time again I was facing disaster and death.

What is more, God was doing this for a purpose. He was looking down through the years to one evening, in October of 1949 when, in Billy Graham's big "Canvas Cathedral" in Los Angeles, I was to accept Christ as my personal Savior. I can see so plainly now that God was sparing my life during these years in order to give me that one last chance.

The first hint of a "charmed life" came when, at two years of age, our house in Los Angles burned to the ground. With the house in flames, my father rushed in, grabbed me from my bed, and carried me to safety just as the building collapsed. But what was supposed to be "me" turned out to be a pillow. Meanwhile I had rolled off and under the bed, and the bed became my temporary protection from the falling embers. Realizing his mistake, my father waded through the hot embers and brought me to safety, but only at the cost to him of burned legs and lifelong scars.

My running career, which was to lead up to the Olympic championship in Berlin in 1936, started when I was four years old. I ran my first race with a playmate down an alley. The other boy won, but just as he drew ahead of me a car hit him, and he was crippled for life. A year and a half later another playmate beat me again in an alley footrace and, again, as in the former race, was hit by a car. This time the boy was killed. Is it not strange that these two early footraces which I lost should have resulted so disastrously for the winners?

After these early "failures" my luck changed, and it just seemed I couldn't lose in my track contests. True, these successes were partly due at least to strenuous efforts on my part—for I was training rigorously three hundred and sixty-five days in the year— but there seemed nevertheless to be that peculiar something, that "charm" that was gravitating me upwards to coveted goals.

In 1934, I broke the high school mile-record with a four minutes and twenty-one and two-tenths seconds. In 1936, at eighteen years of age, I made the U. S. A. Olympic team that competed in Berlin. I was the first American to finish the five thousand meter run. In 1938, while enrolled in the University of Southern California, I set the national collegiate record of four minutes and eight and two-tenth seconds, a record which today, twelve years afterwards, has not yet been bettered.

A near-fatal incident occurred at the Berlin Olympics. A game and adventuresome American youth of eighteen, I wanted to bring along back a souvenir that would be

really different. Adolph Hitler's personal Swastika
would be just that. So, after having competed in the
five thousand meter run, I went into Berlin to find that
flag. There it was, shooting out from the wall from in
front of the chancellery in Berlin. I bounded up the
wall to the flagpole but I couldn't quite reach the flag.
At the same time two guards spotted me. They shouted;
then I saw them raise their rifles. I jumped as high as
I could, clutched the flag in my fist and, as I was falling
to the pavement below, I heard two shots whiz over my
head. Only the fact that I was falling prevented my
having two more holes in my head.

When I hit the ground, twenty feet below, I was
seized and roughly manhandled by the soldiers until
they learned that I was an Olympic runner. Hitler
smiled approvingly at the daring feat, and the soldiers
let me retain the Swastika. I still have that souvenir
among my prized possessions, and every time I look at
it I can hear the zing of bullets.

These, then, have been the more spectacular of the
miracles to the year 1940. I had been aware of the
unusualness of the incidents, but had not attached particular significance to them. Now there began such a
series of unbelievable events as caused me to recognize
beyond the shadow of a doubt that the hand of a
Supreme Being time and again interfered with the
course of nature for my protection. Looked at from
any angle, the facts should have given only one verdict
— DEATH. Yet here I am, by the grace of God,
ALIVE, the only man ever to collect the life insurance
on his own "death."

It all started in the South Pacific. I was one of a crew of ten in a B-24 when, through failure of one of the motors, it crashed into the ocean. The plane exploded upon impact. Seven of the crew were killed instantly. The pilot and the tail-gunner were thrown free, while I found myself pinned tightly under the gun-mount of the plane. The wreckage started to sink rapidly and, of course, I within it.

I lost consciousness at what must have been a depth of fifty feet. For moments there was a complete blackout. Then I regained consciousness and found myself entirely freed from the gun-mount. With a strength that was not merely human I pushed myself downward and out the window of the sinking wrecked plane, inflated my life jacket, and shot towards the surface. There my two companions-in-luck were hanging onto a gas tank. I saw a life raft drifting by me, which had ejected automatically from the plane. I pulled myself aboard and pulled my two buddies in. Not until I was safe in the raft did I discover that I was completely uninjured.

How I became free from the gun-mount; how, after being free, I was able to get out from under the wreckage which was sinking faster than I could swim; what it was that restored me to consciousness even while the water pressure was getting greater; and how all this could happen without leaving a scratch on my body— these are providences that shall forever remain mysteries in my human thinking.

Thus began what was to be for two of the three survivors a forty-seven-day, two-thousand-mile drift on a rubber raft.

Fourteen days passed before any food came our way. The albatross landed on our heads and, in their desperation to get free, would tear our skin off with their saw-tooth bills. Finally we were able to grab one with our bare hands. Quickly we wrung its neck, but the odor of the raw flesh was so putrid that, hungry as we were, we threw the bird away. We did eat a little of the second, for we were hungrier by several days, but most of it went overboard too. By the time we captured the third, we devoured all of it, and when, still later we got a fourth, we picked the bones and relished every morsel.

The fastidiousness of our taste for raw fish disappeared likewise. At first we took only a bite, but toward the end we ate the whole fish, including brains and eyes.

The twenty-seventh day on the raft, another miracle happened. High above us we saw a plane. We sent up a flare. Imagine our unbounded joy when we saw that plane descend in broad spirals to take us, as we thought, out of this wilderness of salt water and boiling sun. Imagine, again, our utter dismay when we saw the identifications of a Japanese plane and heard the rat-a-tat-tat of three machine guns, the business ends of which were pointed toward our rubber boat.

Remembering from my training instruction that bullets will not pierce beyond two and a half feet of water, I got out of and under the raft, holding myself at arm's length beneath the water. My companions remained in the boat, one at each end. For an hour and a half that plane made passes at us, coming down to within a hundred feet, guns blazing all the while.

And while the plane was making passes at us from the air, sharks were making passes at me under the water. I had been told while in training that as a last resort sharks could be scared away by staring at them under water with wide-open eyes. I not only stared at them, but also made faces and stuck out my tongue. It worked! They had no taste for such a hideous looking creature.

During the hour and a half of constant strafing by that Japanese plane, every square foot of our rubber raft was punctured by bullets, and yet not one of us was even grazed. Many bullets did come through the boat directly above me but had spent their force before reaching my head. Before leaving, just to make sure of a thorough job, the plane dropped a depth bomb and then returned to its course. The bomb was a near-miss, and we remained unscathed. As I crawled back into the boat, all three of us joined in a chorus of curses on the so-called human beings in that plane who would treat us so dastardly in our helpless condition.

It took us eight days to patch the punctures in our rubber boat. Every fifteen minutes, day and night, we had to pump air into the raft. We spent an entire day in getting our last patch to stick.

You see, as the days passed we became constantly weaker, and the smallest task called forth a herculean effort. Hunger and thirst and brine and burning sun whittled down both our bodies and our strength, so that I had only seventy of my original hundred and sixty-eight pounds left. Our sun-baked skin came loose in shreds and exposed the bone beneath; for, you see, in many places there was no flesh between.

Once we lived through a period of twelve days without a drop of water to drink. (The usual limit of endurance is said to be six days.) On the thirteenth day, like Elijah's servant, we saw a cloud as big as a man's hand. It promised to be a typical Southwest Pacific squall, a "quickie" shower that rains itself out in two or three minutes over a comparative pinpoint area. We rowed with all our might to get under that cloud. Exhausted but shouting, we arrived there just as it let loose its cargo of moisture, and captured a several days' supply of water. Later this thing happened twice again. Each time the little cloud held its rain until we had rowed directly underneath, and then yielded up its precious "liqueur."

I had never prayed as hard in my life as I did while we were rowing to get under that first cloud. I promised God that I would lead a better life and think of Him more often if only He would please give us food and water. That we did get water that day, as well as on the other two days, made it obvious that God was answering my prayer. Deep in my heart I could not believe otherwise.

By the time we sighted the fourth squall cloud, we were too exhausted to row to it. We dared not further dissipate our precious remaining strength in such wild rowing. *So the cloud came to us.* And when it stood directly overhead, it rained its three-minute shower and disappeared.

Now let us understand the miracle of this. In an expanse of thousands of square miles of ocean, a tiny cloud drifted in the direction of a particular area of less than a single square mile, distilled its moisture at a precise moment, and dropped its refreshing rain into our raft which was floating within that specific, limited area. That this was mere chance is possible but certainly not probable.

In case anyone should still be inclined to explain the incident by saying that "it just happened that way," let me add the most astonishing fact of all: *That same thing occurred seven times more!* In the days subsequent to that first God-directed shower, whenever we got hard up for water, a little cloud would make its appearance in an otherwise clear sky, move to a position directly above us, and let down a two-or three-days' supply of water.

So God answered my prayer for water a total of ten times; three times He waited until we had rowed under the cloud, and seven times He sent the cloud to us. Without this water we would surely have died.

Contrary to popular opinion, we were never tempted to drink the water in which we floated. Drinking salt water was as far from our minds as eating desert sand. Again, contrary to general belief, we never entertained thoughts of cannibalism, even when hungriest. Writhing in agony from gulped salt water and scheming the life of a fellow-survivor would add excitement to a sea story, but it is not my purpose here to tell a sea story for the telling's sake. I want rather to show how God brought me through these incredible experiences in order that I might have that last opportunity to receive the Lord Jesus Christ as my personal Savior and to yield my life over completely to such a solicitous and loving Heavenly Father.

On the thirty-third day our tail-gunner died. Although we had been giving him a larger share of food and water than we were allowing ourselves, his constitution just could not stand the rigors of a raft life. You see, he had sealed his doom before ever coming onto the raft through a life of dissipation. Although not yet a Christian, I attempted a few rites, and we buried him at sea.

Life continued much the same for the two of us. To keep afloat and to keep alive were our chief concerns. It was always an exciting time when one of us would succeed in grabbing a fish, or when the miracle squall would drop down its refreshment. Sometimes we would sit by the hour and talk about food, going into the minutest details concerning that anticipated banquet dinner. This imaginative pastime did seem to give us a degree of satisfaction.

Finally came that forty-seventh day. ('Way back there on the twenty-seventh day we had considered it an achievement worthy of celebration to match the record of Eddie Rickenbacker, but little had we thought then that we would be drifting for twenty more days.) And with the forty-seventh day came *land!* And shouts of joy! And hope! It is hard to describe the thrill of that hour.

Our joy however was short-lived. Before we could land on any one island a Japanese patrol boat spotted us and we were immediately made prisoners of war. Our forty-seven-day solitary confinement on a rubber raft was exchange for a forty-three-day solitary confinement in a two-by-six-foot hole in the ground on the Island of Kwajalein in the Marshall group.

This hole was worse than the raft had been. The rough coral floor cut through our skins and scraped the protruding bones. You see when one loses ninety-eight pounds of weight, there is no fat nor flesh left to cushion the body. We suffered more and prayed harder in this hole than we had in the boat.

On the third day in that hole and within the same hour, my partner, Captain Russell Phillips—so that he may confirm the story—and I both developed a fever. So intense was the fever that it put us into a state of semi-consciousness, dulling our sense of pain and causing the days to pass rapidly. This was God's answer to our prayer, His opiate for our pain. Not until we were being transferred from that hole to a prison camp in Japan forty days later did the fever leave; and when it did, it left us as suddenly and as simultaneously as it had come. This was the most *obvious* answer to prayer that I had experienced up to that time, for God dimmed us out only as long as we were languishing in that dungeon, *and not an hour longer.*

There was one bright spot in connection with our forty-three days in solitary confinement on Kwaialien Island. On the fourth day a new guard came on duty, and he said when he was left alone with us: "You American Christian . . . me Christian . . . we brothers!" For the rest of the forty-three days, that Japanese soldier took a chance with his own life to help us by bringing us additional food, and to make us more comfortable. Again in Japan, another guard said: "You . . . me . . . Christian brothers"; and that Japanese Christian risked his life daily to bring us radio news.

Had either one of these guards been discovered, he would have been executed immediately.

Had I been a born-again Christian at that time, I would have been able better to reciprocate the kindness of these Japanese Christians. They had been converted through the influence of American missionaries, and they supposed that all Americans were Christians. How sorry I am now that I could not at that time fellowship them in the faith as redeemed brothers in Christ!

I was a Catholic. I had been born and raised a Catholic, but I could not possibly agree with their doctrine, even though I had no knowledge of true Christianity. I believed in God and I prayed to God, and, as you have just read, God answered my prayers. In those tight spots on the raft and in the dungeon I promised God that I would be better and think of Him more often, but I still was ignorant concerning Christ and the plan of salvation. My idea of being a Christian was to do many good deeds. I still remember the good feeling that came over me when one time I gave a bum a quarter; I felt that that act won me considerable credit in the eyes of God.

It is no wonder then that with such a limited religious experience I was unprepared for what was to come. News of our release from the Japanese prison camp had preceded us to the States, and when we arrived at San Francisco that city was prepared with a big reception. It was to them as though we had returned from the dead. (In fact, I had been legally declared dead two and a half years before, and my gold star hung on the Warner Brothers roll of honor.) We were feted and dined and given free entertainment and drinks in every night club in the city. Forty-seven-days-on-a-raft heroes, we became the darlings of the entertainment world. Other cities vied with San Francisco to do us honor: Los Angeles gave us front-page publicity; Hollywood's swanky spots where the stars and the elite held sway, welcomed us with open arms. Nattily dressed in our captain's uniforms, we floated around for two years in this dream world. I came to love it all; it seemed as though I just put my arms around these sinful luxuries. The sea and prison experiences were fast becoming just frightful nightmares. Worst of all, *I completely forgot God and the promises I had made to Him.*

Then came a turning point in my life. Up to this time I had succeeded in everything that I attempted. I had emerged out of the vicissitudes of my early experiences unscathed, I had been constantly successful in my athletic career, and God repeatedly snatched me out of impossible situations. Now the tide turned. Now everything that I put my hand to failed. It was as though God were terribly disappointed and was letting me go my own way. Money that had seemed to pour in during the two lush years just seemed to melt away. I entered into a business partnership and my partner absconded with all that I had invested, including the money from my life insurance. (You see, I had been declared "dead," and I collected the insurance on my own death.) Other business ventures failed in turn. It seemed that during these five years of adversity God was letting me see how helpless I really was without His support and protection. The only fortunate experience in this discouraging picture was when, during a rest trip to Florida, I met and subsequently married the girl

who is now my wife. At that time she was one of
Florida's leading debutantes.

The last and biggest of these business propositions
was proffered me in September, 1949. An official of
the Mexican government, calling on me personally in
Los Angeles, drew up a contract whereby I was to be
the sole American representative to collect a tax of
$2.50 from each of the four hundred thousand Ameri-
cans who annually go fishing in Mexican waters. Of
this fee, I was supposed to retain fifty cents as my
commission. That meant an annual income of two
hundred thousand a year. Here, at last, I thought, is
the golden opportunity to recoup my fortune, and I
signed the contract.

"Can I depend upon the terms of this contract?" I
asked the Mexican representative as he stepped into his
big car to leave.

"Mr. Zamparini," he answered reassuringly, "nothing
could invalidate that contract except my own death, and
you needn't worry about that, for I drive so carefully
that I have never felt the need of taking out insurance."
And with a smile and a wave of the hand he drove off.

The following day as he was nearing his home in
Mexico that man was killed in a head-on collision with
another car.

Thus burst the biggest of my business bubbles.

Mrs. Zamparini was supposed to have accompanied
the representative and his family in their car for a short
visit to Mexico, but at the last moment she had found
that duties in connection with her art class would not
permit her to do so.

90

Is it not strange that at the very hour of collision in Mexico, my wife was sitting in the big "Tent Cathedral" in Los Angeles, listening to the preaching of Evangelist Billy Graham?

She had gone there through curiosity, but that curiosity turned to serious reflections as the Holy Spirit used Billy Graham to show to her her need of salvation and the way to receive it. When the invitation was given my wife went to the prayer room and there found Christ as her personal Savior. How great are God's mercies! At the very hour when she might have become a corpse on a Mexican highway, she was being lifted into a new life in Christ Jesus!

A few days later my wife turned missionary; that was only natural, for when one experiences the joy of the forgiveness of sins and reconciliation to God one always wants to have others experience the same. But my wife knew her man. She didn't say, "Let's go to hear a Protestant preacher." Instead she mentioned rather casually that there was a tall, handsome young man, thirty-two years of age (one year younger than I), in a huge circus tent down at Washington and Hill streets, who was drawing nightly crowds of seven to ten thousand people by lecturing on the science of the Bible. She told me how vividly he described certain Bible stories, dramatizing them with his gesticulations as he spoke.

That evening I attended my first Protestant service. It was all very new to me. I was very much interested, but not particularly impressed.

The next day my good wife—God bless her!—used her practical and godly psychology on me all over again, and by evening had squeezed out my promise to go again and to cancel my plans to attend a show.

As I sat in Billy Graham's tent that second night, the promise I had made to God out there on the Pacific kept coming to my mind. It came with a punch. The Spirit of God seemed to be saying to me: "After all that I have done for you, sparing your life time and again, you have forgotten Me and have been thinking only of your sinful pleasures." I began to feel sinful and selfish and ashamed. Billy Graham was saying that all sinners are lost and on the way to hell, and I knew for certain that I was one of them. Yet I did not want to give up my sins because I loved them so much. How hopeless and impossible my condition seemed to me that night!

But after this message of despair came a message of hope. In the most simple language, Billy Graham said that if we acknowledge our sinfulness to God and really believe in His Son, the Lord Jesus Christ, He would take away that terrible guilty feeling and would give peace and joy in the heart instead. Billy said further that God would break the spell that sin has on us and help us to have victory over temptation. He showed how much God loves us and how He wants us to come to Him. The way to God was made so plain to me there that evening.

Conviction was so strong that I was afraid to say no. When the invitation was given I went to the prayer tent, and there with bitter tears confessed my sinfulness, my selfishness, my ungratefulness, and asked God for Jesus' sake to make me His child. I told God I was willing to let go of my sinful pleasures. I felt so miserable and so ashamed of my past life.

After I had been praying for some time, it seemed that my faith took a fast hold on God's promise. Then a miracle happened. Suddenly the heavy burden of sin rolled off my back and without anyone's telling me I *knew* that I had become a new-born child of God. This was the greatest of all miracles in my life.

The thrill of that moment remains indescribable. What a moment that had been out there on the Pacific when I pressed the cup of cool, fresh water to my lips after a twelve-day thirst! But here I drank of the *eternal water of life* after a lifelong thirst for something that would satisfy. Out there God had miraculously freed me from the plane wreckage as it was bearing me with it to ocean's bottom; here, He freed me by His divine power from my sins that were pushing me into hell. There had been shouts in San Francisco when I returned from the Japanese prison camp, but there were shouts among the angels in heaven when I now came to God as a repentant sinner. Yes, roll all the thrills of my life into one, the sum of them would not be equal to the joy and satisfaction and peace that came into my heart in that prayer tent.

From that night on my life was changed.

I did not make my appearance the next morning to sign up, as planned, for my next business venture, a twenty-thousand-dollar-a-year liquor-distributing franchise. I knew that was not the type of business for a Christian.

I did continue to drink moderately, however, for about a week. Then one day when I opened a bottle of

93

choice champagne for a circle of friends, the stuff tasted surprisingly sour and insipid. I apologized to my guests, but they declared that it was as excellent as any we had ever served. The difference was in me. From that day on, I have had no desire for liquor, in spite of the fact that I had always enjoyed social drinking.

I lost sinful companions as well as sinful habits; there were no longer any common ties to bind us together. The world in which they moved was that of dance and drink, motor cars and moneymaking, races and show places and, as I could no longer find my pleasures in this world of "wine, women, and song," we just naturally drifted apart. They recognized the change and wondered why. Secretly, I know, they were wishing for a similar deliverance, for I have myself experienced the periodical fed-up-ness and disgust which this unreal life of tinsel and make-believe brings.

But I found new friends. And the bond between true Christian believers is ever so much stronger than the bond between worldly friends. It is stronger than even blood ties. Months before I read the words in Luke 8:21 where Jesus says, "My mother and my brethren are those which hear the word of God, and do it," I had found that I could have a closer fellowship with my born-again brothers in Christ than I could with my unsaved relatives. "Blest be the tie that binds our hearts in Christian love!"

The marvel of all these tender and gracious dealings of God's hand in my life is still with me. How ashamed I feel when I think of how I ignored and forgot the loving God who repeatedly snatched me from physical death! How humble, when I contemplate His great mercy that finally saved me from eternal death! How inexpressibly happy at the thought that "Beloved, now are we the sons of God, and it doth not yet appear what we shall be; but we know that when He shall appear we shall be like Him!" And all these mercies are mine *because the Lord Jesus Christ suffered in my place!*

It is no wonder then, that when I was offered fifty thousand dollars a year to tell my life story from the lecture platform I refused; for, had I accepted, I would not have been permitted to mention the name of Christ, and it is in the name of Christ that I glory. Why should I be telling about the many miracles in my life, and not mention the One who has wrought those miracles? How cheap that would be!

No, instead of telling my story for money, I find great satisfaction in telling it to audiences everywhere as a testimony to the saving power of Christ. My compensation and my greatest thrill is to see others accept Christ as their Savior, even as I.

Do not infer that there have been no difficulties in this new Christian life. To say so would be entirely untrue. There has been opposition a-plenty. Satan contests every foot of spiritual progress. But "thanks be to God who giveth us the victory through our Lord Jesus Christ!" The compensations far outweigh the hardships; the sufferings are not to be compared with the glory.

Yes, I am now in the Christian race. Of all my track experiences this is the greatest. Just as when I broke the World's record I stripped myself of all encumbrances, so in this Christian race I have been putting aside the sins and the weights in order that I might run steadily and with patience the course set before me. By the grace of God I expect to win. And when I breast the tape into the presence of Christ I know I shall have such a thrill as shall dwarf my World's record into infantile proportion. I hope to hear from the lips of my Lord Himself the words, "Well done!" And then, while heaven is ringing with the shouts of victory, I shall bow at the feet of my Savior and tell Him personally how sorry I am for having ignored Him so long and how thankful that He took my place and suffered for my sins.

May I urge you who read this not to forget God like I did. Accept Christ as your personal Savior. Get into the Christian race *now,* if you have not already done so. I would like to be at the goal and help shout "Hooray" when you cross the line.

* * *

16 HAVE YOU EVER HAD A STITCH IN YOUR SIDE?

Dr. Hyman J. Appelman thought he was sick. Didn't he lose sixty-two pounds in less than four months! The scene opens with the brilliant and successful young lawyer asking a D.D. to kindly refer him to an M.D. As told in his autobiography, "From Lawyer to Preacher," published by American Association for Jewish Evangelism, Winona Lake, Indiana. By kind permission of both Dr. Appelman and Publisher.

"Doctor," I said, "I don't feel well. I need a physician; I need medical treatment. The YMCA secretary said that you had some good doctors in your church."

"Tell me a little about yourself," he said. "Who are you, and where are you from?"

I told him the story of my life in detail as he asked me many questions, one after another. We started talking at three o'clock in the afternoon, and it was long past midnight when he had finished with me. With all my soul I thank God that that preacher had the grace and the patience to stay with me. He asked me about my father, my mother, my religion, my Lord. He asked what I knew about the Bible, and Judaism, and Christianity. When he had finished, he said, "You don't need a doctor, my boy; you need the Lord Jesus Christ."

I started to leave. "Doctor," I told him, "I am a Jew. I don't believe in the Lord Jesus Christ. I don't need him."

He pressed his hands on my knees to keep me down. I couldn't push the man away, so I sat there. Presently, instead of continuing to talk to me, he walked to the window. On the window seat was one of those little Bibles they use in Sunday School. He picked up that Bible, came over to me, and opened it. He began to read a portion, and then he talked about what he had read. Occasionally he asked me to read, and then he asked me if I understood what I had read. Then he told me the story of the Lord Jesus Christ.

He did not preach; he did not tell me what to believe; he did not draw a moral. For the first time in my life I heard the story of Jesus. (I would not besmirch my lips; I would not defile the Name of our precious Redeemer, by telling you what I had thought of the Lord Jesus Christ until that time.) He told me the story so well, so vividly, so warmly — tears at times would course down his cheeks—that I could almost see and feel the Lord Jesus Christ there in that room.

He told me about the Lord's birth and infant years, of His appearance in the Temple. He told me about His baptism, about His teaching, His preaching, His healing, His miracle-working. He told me about the prayer in Gethsemane and the blood-like sweat; about the cruel cursing in Pilate's judgment hall; about the Cross. He told me about His second coming, and for the first time in my life I heard what I now believe to be the truth—that my people are confusing the second coming of Christ with His first coming. I did not know that the Bible taught two comings, and most of my people still do not know it. The more this man of God told me, the clearer the truth became and the more strongly it sank and burned into my soul. Oh, I do thank God for Mr. Davis, and the warmness and the enthusiasm and the burden of his testimony!

After talking for some time, he stopped and, turning to me, said, "There is one thing that will help you, and nothing else. Will you accept Jesus as your personal Savior?"

I answered, "Preacher, I can't do it; I just can't do it."

"Well," he replied, "there is just one more thing that I can do for you. Will you kneel and pray with me?"

"I do not know how to pray," I answered. "You do not mean for me to pray Hebrew prayers, do you?"

"No," he answered. "I want you to pray from your heart."

"Preacher," I said, "I have never done that in my life. I would not know how to begin."

"Kneel with me," he said, "and I will pray for you."

We dropped to our knees; he put his arm around me and pressed me to himself, and began to pray. His voice was so tender, so broken. I opened my eyes and began to study him. Great beads of perspiration stood out on his forehead. Great tears coursed down his cheeks. I could not understand how anyone who had met me for the first time that day could be so concerned about me. Thank God, I understand now, for I, too, have wept my soul out, times without number, for the souls of men.

When he had concluded his prayer, he turned to me. My heart was in my throat. I did not know what to do. I wanted to jump up and run out of that room. I was so torn and disturbed and unhappy. The devil was putting up his last fight to keep me from accepting Christ.

Still with his arm around me, the pastor asked, "Will you accept and confess Christ as your personal Savior?"

"Preacher," I said, "I can't do it; I just can not do it."

"Why not?"

I was almost hysterical. I said, "I'll tell you why. You have been honest with me; I will be honest with you. I have a father and a mother and four brothers and a sister. I am the oldest son. My father has bankrupted himself to help me. My mother has slaved away her days to help me. If I give my heart to Christ, it will break their hearts and bring them to their graves."

99

He said, "I know. I understand. But think what the Lord Jesus Christ has done for you. After all, He loved you, too, and He not only lived for you, but He *died* for you,"—and he continued to press the Cross upon me.

It is hard to tell it even now, heartbreaking to tell it, but then it was a soul-crushing experience. I would take a long look at Jesus stretched out on the Cross for my sins, and between Him and me would be the faces of my father and my mother. I would take a long look at their dear faces—oh, how I loved them, and how I love them still!—and standing between them and me would be the Cross of my Redeemer.

The preacher was praying and crying, and I began to cry, too. Surely the Holy Spirit came to my help. I was honest; I was sincere; I was truly trying to find the truth.

Presently there came an ease in my heart, a kind of looseness.

"Preacher," I said, "when you say 'accept Christ,' what do you mean?"

He opened the Bible again, and turned to Romans 10:9, the first verse I ever memorized; I memorized it right then and there on my knees in that parlor room. He read it to me: "That if thou shalt confess with thy mouth the Lord Jesus, and shalt believe in thine heart that God hath raised him from the dead, thou shalt be saved."

He said, "Do you understand it?"

"Not quite," I replied.

"Well, you read it," he said, which I did. Then he added, "Read it out loud." I read it again and again, about four or five times, and by that time I knew it from memory.

"Do you understand it now?" he asked.

"Well," I answered, "what does it mean to 'confess Christ'?"

"Let me ask you some questions," he said. "Do you believe that Jesus Christ died for your sins?"

I countered with, "Do *you* believe it?"

His answer was "Yes."

"Why do you believe it?" I said.

"Because the Bible says so," he answered.

To which I replied, "Well, I believe it, too."

And somehow I did believe it. I could not understand why then, but I do now. John 7:17 says, "If any man will do his will, he shall know of the doctrine, whether it be of God; or whether I speak of myself." If you have any doubt about some verse of Scripture that contains a definite commandment of God, just say to Him, "Lord, I will do whatever it teaches me to do," and God will open it to you, and explain it to you. He did that for me right there while I was on my knees.

I said, "I believe Jesus Christ died for my sin because you believe it and the Book says so."

"Now, do you believe that God raised Christ from the dead?" the pastor asked me.

I said, "Do you believe it?"

Again his answer was, "Yes."

"Why do you believe it?" I asked.

And again his answer was, "Because the Bible says so."

"I believe it, too," I declared, "because you say so

101

and the Bible says so," and somehow, thank God, and glory be to Christ, I did believe it.

Then he asked, "Will you confess Christ as your personal Savior?"

"You still have not told me what it means to confess Christ as my personal Savior," I reminded him.

"Will you ask God, for Christ's sake, to forgive your sins? That is all."

His arm was still around me, my body pressed close to his. I closed my eyes. My heart was full. My soul was torn within me. I wanted to cry, and cry hard. I bit my lips until somehow I got control of myself.

Then I lifted my face to God, and through my clenched teeth I said, "Lord, I do not know, and I do not understand, but this man says this Book says that Your Son died for my sins, and that if I ask You to, for His sake, You will forgive my sins. Lord, for Christ's sake, do forgive my sins."

Have you ever had your sides taped? I have. I was thrown from a horse one time when I was a boy, and the horse stumbled on me and almost killed me. For days I wore a kind of strait jacket. I remember the day it was taken off, and what a relief that was! Have you ever had a stitch in your side, so that it seemed you had to breathe by jerks? Then, suddenly, the stitch was gone and you could take a deep breath without pain. What a relief that was!

Well, that is exactly the way I felt after I had prayed to God to save me for Christ's sake. God did, for Christ's sake, forgive my sins then and there. Then and there the burden was lifted. Then and there I found the satisfaction I had long longed for.

17   **MR. CHENG OF SHENSI**

Story by G. Reuben Gustafson, long-time missionary in Kienyang, Shensi, China; associated with the Evangelical Alliance Mission.

Some years ago in a conference in Kienyang, Shensi, the meetings were especially blessed of God. One day an official of the Government entered the church and sat on the rear bench. We could see that he was definitely moved. Tears were running down his cheeks. Someone said that we should approach him and ask him if he wished us to pray. Others said the Holy Spirit was working in his heart and he would come again.

The next day he sat in the middle portion of the church, and again tears were running down his cheeks.

On the third day he was sitting on the front bench, drinking in everything that was being said. And on this day, when the invitation was given, this dear man stood up and with tears streaming down his face said that he wanted to believe in Christ.

When we asked him why he wanted to believe in Christ he replied that he realized he was a sinner, and that he wanted to be saved and have the joy that we had. He said that when he had money he had many friends, but when he had no money he had no friends. Then he asked us to come down to his house and help him to pray that he would have victory over his bad habits, such as cigarettes and opium. Also he wanted to have help to throw out the idols in his home.

With these requests we were happy to comply, for it was always a special joy to seize every opportunity to destroy the idols which keep so many of the Chinese people in fear and superstition.

Mr. Cheng—that was the name of this Government official—was a tax collector, and, like Matthew of old, he gave up his business and followed Jesus wholly. It was not long before his wife and daughter had also accepted Christ. His wife remarked that she had received a new husband; he did not beat her as he had done formerly.

Although a Government tax collector, Mr. Cheng had not been able to read or write. Now that he had become a Christian he wanted to read the Bible and one could see each evening his daughter sitting on the mud bed in their home, teaching her father to read.

Later this Chinese saint became an elder in the church. Like Matthew the Apostle, he and all his family became faithful and fruitful followers of the Master.

* * *

18   A BLACKSKIN'S HEART MADE WHITE

The conversion of Timothy Nzenge, of the Banjavis tribe in the district of Gabon, near the great bend on the African coast, is typical of the power of the gospel to change the life of the raw native. It happened at a newly-established mission station of the Christian and Missionary Alliance, and is authenticated by that organization.

When the missionary came to his country, Timothy Nzenge was already grown and in possession of three wives, two of whom were inherited from a deceased uncle, and the third, a young girl of about twelve years, whom he had married of his own choice.

His father had been taken away into slavery when he was a small lad, and the boy never saw him again.

He eventually learned to make his living by forging knives and spears or carving dance masks. In his little bark hut were hung the usual fetishes to ward off illness, a spear thrust into the top of the one doorway, pointing down, to frighten away any evil spirits that might try to enter. In one corner was a cooking pot filled with the decayed bodies of twin babies mixed with a white clay from the river bottom. Into this mixture the unfortunate mother of the twins had to dip her finger, rubbing some on each breast and on her forehead before leaving her house, bearing always the curse for having given birth to a divided soul (one soul in two bodies which must be reunited by death).

Timothy appeared one day at the mission and asked for work. He later revealed that his real purpose in coming was in order to hear as often as possible the wonderful new story of God's love, brought by the missionaries to his land.

He was hired to make knives and spears, whereupon he set up his little forge at one end of the dirt floor verandah. For some time he worked there, observing these strange people, listening attentively to their messages, and pondering in his heart the things he saw and heard.

Finally under deep conviction for his sins and in sincere repentance, he accepted Christ as his Savior. His fetishes, including the clay pot with the bodies of his twins, were destroyed. His inherited wives were put away, and his life was completely changed by the power of God as he sought to become a true follower of his Lord.

God's blessing has been in evidence in his life and ministry, and he is being greatly used in the necessary translation work done in the Banjavis tribal language. He is a discerning church elder and a faithful supervisor of a large group of native workers.

* * *

19   I DID NOT WANT TO EMBARRASS THE LORD

In C. O. Baptista, who has pioneered in the field of religious films, is found the rare combination of mechanical skill, dramatic art, and a passion for souls. From his studio in Wheaton, Illinois, have come many fine films. He permits no one who is not a Christian to participate in his productions. Here is the story of his own conversion.

It is a strange feeling to come to the United States from a foreign country to make one's fortune and find one's self alone and friendless in a big city, with only hopes and dreams of what he might become in the distant future.

A young man of nineteen, I arrived in Chicago with a few hundred dollars in my pocket. I thought that I was rich and that I could never be in need.

I found a job with a company that manufactured pianos. It wasn't hard to get the job, for I promised to create an export business for them and told them they did not have to pay me a salary since I was financially independent (I thought that my money would last a long time); I would work entirely on a commission basis.

On the Monday morning when my job started, they provided a little desk for me in the middle of a long and gloomy room.

It was well that I did not know then how hard it was going to be to sell pianos by mail in foreign countries. But hope kept me buoyant.

Three months after starting to work I had not sold a single piano.

One Sunday evening while I was having supper in a crowded cafeteria in Chicago's downtown, a man at the same table engaged me in friendly conversation and among other things asked me about my religion. I told him that I was a Roman Catholic. Then he asked me if I believed that the Pope could forgive sins. I replied that I did not understand how he could. Before the man said goodby he handed me a little book and told me it was the most remarkable book in all the world, and that a person would not be the same after having read it.

The next day was Sunday. Instead of going to mass as was my custom I stayed in bed and read the little book; and just as the man had said, there came a peculiar feeling, and that despite the fact that the English language was still difficult for me.

One verse stood out. It was the one where the Lord says that He would do anything that we would ask in His name. That statement seemed remarkable to me; for if the Lord said it, then those words must be true; otherwise the Lord would be false.

As the weeks went on without my selling any pianos, and as my money was rapidly disappearing, I began to worry. Still friendless and alone in the big city, not knowing what to do, and ashamed to write home for help, the words of the little book returned to me, and one night I did not say my prayers in the usual manner. Instead of repeating a set prayer without thinking of the meaning, I talked plainly to God, telling Him of my predicament, how that my money was almost gone, and asking Him if He would not be good enough to help me. Then a very peaceful feeling came over me, as if a guardian angel were saying to me, "Don't worry; God will take care of you."

Next day the first order for a piano came from South America. I was overcome with joy and thanked God, but still was not sure whether it was an answer to my prayer or a mere coincidence.

If it were really God's answer, would it not be wonderful to keep praying and getting orders? How much I wanted to pray for more sales! And yet I was afraid to ask for more because I did not want to catch God unawares or to embarrass Him when He could not fulfill my petition. So I waited until one night when I felt constrained to pray again. The next day another order arrived.

Then I began to pray to God daily, not always for sales, but whenever I did pray about my business, an order always came, thus convincing me that it was really the Lord who heard my prayers and granted my requests.

More and more I was thinking about the Lord. A certain man at the piano company often came to my desk and told me about Jesus, and he told me that it *is* true that the little book which had been given to me in the restaurant had power and life unlike other ordinary books which we read.

On Sundays I continued going to mass, but my hunger for the things of God was not satisfied. Up to then I thought that Protestant churches were evil places and I would not even walk past them. How surprised I was therefore when one Sunday I found myself inside the Buena Memorial Presbyterian Church in Chicago. It had not been my intention to go there, but being inside, and finding myself cordially greeted by friendly people, I decided to stay for the service.

They explained to me more clearly about the Lord Jesus Christ—the same Lord mentioned in the little Book of John. And there, that day, He became my Savior and the Lord of my Life.

Just think what the Lord has done for me! He called me, He saved me, He sent the Holy Spirit to live in me, and has given me the joy and privilege of serving Him. He is Director of my life, my business, and my home. He has given me peace of mind, contentment, and joy. He has forgiven me of my sins and shortcomings and has given me eternal life. All my needs, physical, mental, and spiritual, are provided. I do not want for anything; my cup runs over.

* * *

20   **SOBERED AND SAVED**

This experience, prepared by Tom M. Olson, one of the most prolific of tract writers, is here presented as an evidence that God controls the efforts of tract evangelism. From "Tracts," by permission of the Tract Club of America.

Many people believe that their circumstances hinder them from spreading the gospel of Christ. A woman, sixty-nine years of age, has written telling me of some of her experiences. Her husband is over seventy, and on account of a broken leg had been laid up for months. But she had a class of boys in her home every Monday afternoon, and whenever possible she would go to a little mission in the town. She writes:

One night only a few people came to the mission and I felt I had accomplished so little for my Master. So I decided to go to the street corner with a packet of tracts. Carefully and prayerfully I handed them to passersby.

One man came along who was very much under the influence of liquor. I handed him a tract. He took it, crossed the street, and then leaned against a fence and tried to read the tract under a light on that corner. It was a very dark night.

Just then I saw two policemen coming along. At once I prayed God to speedily get me across the street where I could protect this man so he would not be arrested. I wanted him to continue reading that gospel tract. I reached him quickly and shielded him as the police passed. They apparently did not notice him.

Then I spoke to the man: "Do you understand the tract you are reading?"

He looked up, recognizing me as the one who had given him the tract. "Yes," he said, "I understand it. It says: 'Where will you spend eternity?'"

When I asked him where he did expect to spend it, he said: "In hell, unless I am saved now!"

"Do you really want to be saved now?" I asked him.

"Yes, lady, I do."

It was a joy to give him the gospel in simplicity. I then said to him, "The Bible says, 'Today if ye hear His voice, harden not your heart.' It also says, 'Now is the accepted time; now is the day of salvation.' Will you accept Him? Will you believe Him *now?*"

"Yes, I will," he said.

Then I said to him, "Let's bow our heads and tell the Lord Jesus all about it." We prayed by that fence, and when I raised my head I realized that God had sobered and saved that man. He took my hand to thank me.

I told him that I was only a vessel for God to use and that he should ever thank God who gave His only begotten Son in order that we might be saved.

I asked him where he lived. He said he lived in Newark, New Jersey. He added, "I could not go to work today. It seemed as though something told me I must go to Scranton (Pennsylvania) and the pull was so irresistible that I took the bus and came. God had to send me here from Newark to get this tract and it will never leave me now."

He told me that he had a brother just outside Scranton, who was a Christian and who had often pleaded with him to accept Jesus Christ as his personal Savior, but he would never yield to his brother's entreaties.

"Now," he said, "I am going to go and tell him. It is only a twenty-minute walk from here." He left, thanking me profusely for the tract that had been given him at the right time under the guidance of God.

How I wished I had had a car to take him to his brother's place and witness the meeting!

* * *

21   **HE DIDN'T HAVE A CLEAN SOLE**

Leland Wang has been called the D. L. Moody of China. As this article well reflects, Rev. Wang's concern has been for his people, both on the mainland of China and in the South Sea Islands.

"Come and hear, all ye that fear God, and I will declare what He hath done for my soul." (Psalm 66:16)

I was brought up in a home in Foochow where two hundred people lived together in a compound. None of them were Christians. I never went to a Sunday school or mission when I was a boy, and the first Bible that ever came into my hands was one given to my father by a Christian friend. He did not read it. One day I saw this beautiful book on his desk and said, "Father, may I have that Book?" He said, "Yes." I began to read it but could not understand a word, and I thought it was a useless book. As a boy I liked to collect postage stamps, and so I used my first Bible as a stamp album.

I want to tell you one or two stories of the days of my youth, so that you will have some idea of the background of my life. If anyone treated me well, I liked him; if he did not treat me well, I hated him. Once when I was staying with my uncle, my mother's brother, he spanked me, so I did not like him. I wished he might have a headache or a stomach-ache, then I would be happy. But he was as well as could be. One day I asked somebody what would happen if I drank kerosene oil. I was told it would make me sick. So I stole some of the oil and poured it into my uncle's rice. But my uncle had a nose; he could smell it before he ate, and he asked, "Why is there oil in my rice?" Someone said, "This boy has been asking if he might drink oil, so he must be the guilty one."

Our family owned a shop in Foochow and when money was taken—silver or paper—it was put into a big receiving box at the back of the shop; but when pennies were taken, the same care was not used and the coppers would sometimes fall onto the floor. As a boy, this was a great temptation to me. I thought, If I ask for pennies for my candies perhaps they won't give them to me; so I will try to get them myself. I put some paste on the bottom of my shoes and then walked about the shop, and came out with the pennies sticking onto the bottom of my shoes, as many as I wanted. I thought that as I did not pick the pennies up, I did not steal. I had a clear conscience, but I did not have a clean *sole*.

When I was fourteen years old, I went to Shanghai to study in a Government school, but there was no Bible teaching there. One day I had an accident. I fell from a high place and broke my leg, and had to lay in hospital for a month. During that time I began to study religion—Buddhism, Confucianism, Taoism—but none of them gave me satisfaction.

About two years later I went to Chefoo, and while there I began to think on life and its problems. Thinking that I could not solve any of these problems, I began to seek the pleasures of sin, drinking and gambling and so forth. But none of these gave me joy.

When I had finished my schooling I came to Woosong where I became engaged to be married. My fiancee was not a Christian at that time, but one day, to my surprise, I received a letter from her, telling me that she had been converted in a gospel meeting held in her college (Hunan Women's College, Foochow), conducted by Miss Ruth Paxson, and she asked me to go to some church nearby to hear the gospel. When I read her letter I was disappointed, and wrote to her saying, "I have no time to go to church, and, I want to be frank with you, I do not care to go." This was my first attitude toward Christianity. But God was able to change that.

Shortly after that I came back to Foochow and my parents arranged our wedding. We wished to use the chapel of the Women's College but the principal sent a message to say that if we did so, we must have a Christian wedding. So, although I was not a Christian, we had a Christian wedding. When the pastor came with his Bible under his arm, he said to me, "You need not do anything, Mr. Wang. I will ask you a few questions and you just nod your head." After he had read the Scripture, he asked us all to stand in prayer. I had never been to a prayer meeting, so I watched to see how the people prayed. I saw that some had their eyes closed and some had their eyes open; I stood with one eye open and one eye shut! That was my first experience of prayer.

After the ceremony we went home. According to Chinese custom, the bride and bridegroom must bow to the ancestors; but my wife refused to do this on the ground that she was a Christian. I was not pleased with her, neither were my parents; and I went myself and bowed. Today I am glad that my wife took that stand, because now all my family are Christians; if she had bowed, there would have been a different story.

A few days later, on Sunday, my wife asked me to go with her to church. I went, and although I could not understand a word the preacher said, I was greatly impressed with the last hymn, *Nearer My God to Thee.* I thought that if these people want to get near to the God whom they worship, they must have a wonderful God. People who worship idols are afraid of them. If you were to say, "The idol be with you," they would be scared. But these Christians seemed to be comforted by the words, "God be with you."

After the service the people shook hands with me and said they hoped to see me next Sunday. My wife said, "Mr. Wang is not a Christian yet; please pray for him." My wife told me that she had asked many people to pray for me. I said to myself I would wait and see whether God answered their prayers. At that time I thought that prayer was superstition, but now I know it is fellowship with God.

One day when I was walking along the street, I began to think how Christianity had come to China over a hundred years ago, how schools have been opened for children, and hospitals for the sick, and homes for the lepers. I reasoned that Christians are doing much good in my country and, since the fruits are good, the tree must be good; and Jesus Christ must be a good Man. Then I remembered that the history of this world is dated either before or after the birth of Jesus; why was not some other outstanding person in history chosen? I decided that by all means I must know the life story of Jesus.

I was told that if I wanted to know about Jesus the best Book to read was the Bible—but not the Old Testament, for that would be too hard. So I started with the New Testament, the first chapter of Matthew's Gospel: "Abraham begat Isaac; and Isaac begat Jacob . . . ," and I was discouraged because these names were not interesting to me. But I read on, and came to the place where Jesus said, "Blessed are the pure in heart: for they shall see God." I said to myself, How can I expect to see God? I know the condition of my own heart too well. Then again I read, "When thou doest alms, let not thy left hand know what thy right hand doeth." And I thought, if I do something good I like people to know it and to talk about it, the more the better.

So the teaching of Jesus began to draw my attention. The more I read the story of the gospel the more I realized that there must be a living and true God. Then I began to see that Jesus Christ, the Son of God, was the Mediator between God and me; that He died for my sins on the cross; and that He is able to save to the uttermost all those that come to God through Him.

Thus it was that in 1918 I took the Lord Jesus Christ as my personal Savior.

After I was saved I became deeply concerned over the salvation of my family. Praise the Lord for the promise, "Believe on the Lord Jesus Christ and thou shalt be saved *and thy house.*" So I began to pray for my mother, and she was the first one to come to the Lord in answer to prayer. Then afterwards my brother Wilson came to the Lord, and he is now a preacher of

116

the gospel. Then my two younger brothers, and finally my father, all came to the Lord. Recently my uncle (the one to whom I gave the oil) came to the Savior before he died. Praise God for His marvelous salvation!

Reading God's Word has been a great blessing in my spiritual life. One day I read these words in Acts 17:11: " . . . they searched the scriptures *daily*," . . . and I decided to do the same thing by God's help. My motto for years has been, *No Bible, no breakfast;* because I realize that I must "seek first the kingdom of God and his righteousness."

In 1920 I was baptized by immersion in obedience to the Lord's Word. Then in 1921 the Lord called me to preach. One day as I was reading the Bible my thoughts were directed to Isaiah 52:11, 12: "Depart ye, depart ye, go ye out from thence . . . for the Lord will go before you; and the God of Israel will be your reward." I felt that the Lord wanted me to be "separated unto the gospel," and I gladly obeyed His call.

The problem of the support of my family was brought up; I could not ask my father to support me. One evening a missionary invited me to her home and gave me the *Life of George Muller* of Bristol. I read it with great interest. I said to myself, "George Muller did not go round to raise money for his orphans, and since God is no respecter of persons, He can answer my prayers too." Besides there was the example of how God supplied the needs of two million people, including women and children, in the wilderness for forty years, and it came to me that God could easily take care of a small family. So I decided to trust the Lord to supply *all* my needs according to Philippians 4:19.

I went back to Foochow and started open-air meetings. I used to take a bell and a basket full of tracts and Gospels, and go out on the streets where crowds would gather around and listen while I sang and preached the gospel. It is a great joy to see sinners come to Jesus, the manifestation of the power of the gospel in saving souls.

The Lord has marvelously opened the door for His unworthy servant to preach in different parts of China. In 1928 He called me to go to the South Sea Islands. After a tour I returned and told the churches in China about the need of the gospel in those Islands, and we have sent out twelve Chinese missionaries since then to preach the gospel to the Chinese people there as well as to the natives. The Lord has graciously blessed that work in the salvation of souls.

* * *

22   **HITCH-HIKING FOR CHRIST**

Out of the experience which Herb Seal here narrates, grew his "Sixty Thousand Miracle Miles" of highway evangelism, with a surprising harvest of many souls won for Christ. He is founder and national director of the American Revival Campaign, Inc.

It was as a high school student that for the first time I attended Percy Crawford's Pinebrook Youth Conference. At the last service of that conference the missionary was giving us a vision of the hopeless condition of those who had never even heard the name of Christ. At that time I felt no call to the mission field nor to the ministry; but I did want to do something and so I gave the couple of dollars I had saved for my bus fare home.

The thought came, "That was a silly trick. Now you are broke!"

Then the Lord called to my mind these words: "I will supply all your needs according to My riches in glory through Christ Jesus." A real peace came upon me and I worried not a bit.

My luggage and I were waiting around after the service, not knowing exactly what to do when all of a sudden I thought, "I'll hitch-hike home!"

The driver of the conference station wagon asked me, "What train are you catching?"

"I'm not taking the train," I replied.

"Oh, what bus then?"

"I'm not taking a bus, either."

"How are you going?"

"I'm supposed to get a ride from Stroudsburg in a private car."

"I'll take you to town then," he said. "Hop in."

He left me at the main corner, and I began waiting for that "private car." Soon a car that wasn't exactly private (although at times it did offer exclusive rides to certain travelers!) drove up alongside me. It was a white State Police car, and the officer asked from where I had come.

"From Pinebrook Bible Conference, sir," I said.

"I guess you are O.K.," he said; "but let me give you a hint. You can pick up rides easier if you go to the traffic light down by the bridge."

"Thank you, sir," I replied, and picking up my luggage walked over to the more desirable spot.

I was standing at this point only a few minutes when along came my private car—a forty-foot coal truck. One could not be fussy in my position, so I accepted the proffered lift.

"Where are you headed for?" asked the colored driver after we had gotten under way.

"Heaven, sir," I answered, and added quickly, "Are you going there?"

"Well now I'd like to," he said, "but not right yet. You see I've got to get to New York."

I told my colored friend he should be getting on the road to heaven at once and I tried to show him the way.

"First," I said, "you must want to get rid of your sins. You don't want to ask God to forgive your sins if you are going to continue in them. You must be really sorry for all the wicked things you have done."

"You're right, son," he reflected seriously. "But what do I do next?"

I quoted the words of Acts 16:31: "Believe on the Lord Jesus Christ and thou shalt be saved." "You must believe *with your heart*," I added, "and not only with your head. You believe in George Washington, but you have never met him personally. When you believe in Christ you must meet Him personally, in your heart. Do you see what I mean?"

"Yes, sir, I think I do," the driver said seriously. "I would really like to believe and to know that I am going to heaven like you do."

We talked further about how to be saved and before we knew it we were in New Plainfield. Before I got out, the driver pulled to the side of the road and we bowed our heads together in prayer. When we raised our heads again I saw that his black face, although streaked with tears, showed a glow of joy. I felt sure that he had met the Lord in forgiving mercy and that he now too was on the road to heaven.

* * *

23 SEE WHAT SIN DOES; SEE WHAT CHRIST DOES!

Here are bare facts only; you must read between the lines the misery and the suffering of a sinful life. J. A. Peabody is ashamed of this black record. He tells it only to show how powerful is the Christ who can deliver completely from such a dark past. Upon inquiry just before going to press, it was found that he is still living a victorious Christian life.

My father died when I was only six. My mother was a Christian and prayed for her boy, but she died when I was eleven years old. I went to live with an uncle who was a cowboy preacher. When fifteen years old I left his home to shift for myself. I was headstrong and resisted all religious appeals. I began to drift, got work on a construction gang, learned to drink, and kept bad company. Drinking led to dope, then stealing. My life went from bad to worse until I was given twenty years in "the Big House" for assault and robbery. I was released after nine years and nine months. Some time later I was put in again for two years.

I came to Los Angeles about twenty years ago. Soon found myself a "wino" on Skid Row. I have been in Lincoln Heights jail more than seventy-five times for drunkenness, panhandling, using and peddling dope. Whether I was guilty or not, the police searched my room periodically just to watch me. I was often accused of crime I was not guilty of. I spent two years in solitary confinement for selling dope.

My health was gone. I was helpless to quit drinking. I landed in the hospital twenty times with delirium tremens. They would strap me down, and oh, how I would suffer! I was not fit to live and I did not die. In my last drunken spree I set fire to my room. I landed in jail again. This time I became very sick and tired of my life. I was at the end of myself. I prayed for God to save me. I confessed my sins. *God saved me and forgave my sins and helped me to quit my sinful life!*

But I still felt weak and powerless to face the old temptations. One evening at Peniel Hall, in Los Angeles, I received this strength. The Holy Spirit went through me like a warm streak of electricity, and then I had power over all sin.

He has kept me now for seven years from going back into my old life. It is wonderful to be a Christian!

* * *

24 **BOBBY**

J. C. Brumfield is director of the Radio Kids Bible Club, which is the Radio Voice of the International Child Evangelism Fellowship, and vice president of the International Child Evangelism Fellowship. His program is released coast to coast in this country and in many foreign countries. He is also author of the widely-read Susie Books.

Bobby came to us from an orphans' home when he **was four** years of age. He was sweet and he was intelligent, but surely it could not be said that he had any "background." He had had no opportunities for Christian teaching and instruction, and it was only with the assurance that the grace of God can overcome any possible hereditary "taint" that we proudly took him as our own little boy.

Bobby had been with us only a few weeks when he attended a revival campaign which I was conducting in our city. Each evening as I gave the invitation for those who were concerned to raise their hands, little Bobby raised his high. There were those who smiled at this, and it seemed to hinder the service at the crucial moment. I explained very tactfully that raising his hand was very disturbing and that he should not do it again. With a perplexed look on his face, he said, "But Daddy, you asked us to." "I didn't mean *you*," I replied, not thinking it possible that God was actually speaking to the heart of this four-year-old.

Despite our warning, Bobby continued raising his hand. Once when he thought I had not seen his hand, he got far out into the aisle and waved his hand. Mother was at the piano and could not correct him. It was evident that this act attracted the attention of some who had been deeply under conviction. Bobby was soundly spanked when he got home that night.

A few days later, I had to go out of town for a week of meetings. Mother was ill, and the girl who had been working in our home was suddenly called away. There was nothing left to do but to take Bobby with me.

One night Bobby came to the prayer room with a number of other seekers. As I was dealing with the seekers, Bobby was crying and hanging on my neck so much that he became a hindrance. I asked the pastor's wife to take him out of the room. Somehow he got away from her, and was soon back again. Again I sent him out with orders not to return.

That night I read to him the usual Bible story before going to bed. The story was about Calvary. In simple words I explained the facts concerning the trial, crucifixion and death of Jesus "for our sins." I turned the light out and was nearly asleep when suddenly in the darkness Bobby surprised me by asking, "Daddy, doesn't Jesus love me like He loved those other little children tonight?" I assured him that Jesus did. Then he said in a perplexed tone, "Well, Daddy don't *you* love me like you loved those other little children?" I assured him that I loved him and told him to go to sleep. He answered, "But you didn't tell me how to be saved. You didn't pray with me like you prayed with those other little children."

I turned on the light. Bobby's eyes were swimming in tears. I dealt with him for half an hour, asking him questions that would be embarrassing to many adults. It was evident that he was feeling his need of salvation. I said, "Bobby, do you want to trust Jesus as your Savior?" He said, "Yes." I said, "When?" He replied, "Right now." And with that he climbed over me and lit on his knees on the floor. You should have heard that little boy pray! He has given every evidence of having been genuinely born again.

I tell this story in humility and shame, and with an appeal to other parents to be ever watchful for indications of the Lord's dealing with their "little ones."

Yes, *"little* children" need to be saved; they can be saved; they should be saved; they must be saved before "the evil days come . . ." and it is forever too late!

* * *

25 BELIEVE THE INSTRUMENTS; IGNORE YOUR FEELINGS

James C. Truxton is founder and president of the Missionary Aviation Fellowship, an organization of a dozen Christian aviators who give their services in flying missionaries to and from their mission fields.

Aunt Verna came to stay with us during a period of illness in our family. Those days have remained with me as a warm and happy memory, for Aunt Verna was living before me—living ever so beautifully—the first vital Christian witness I had ever experienced. I found myself longing to know the secret of her deep joy and serenity.

In those days I had grave intellectual doubts regarding the authenticity and the authority of the Bible. I wanted to bring my problems to Aunt Verna, but would hesitate at the last moment, for I somehow sensed what her answer would be. I therefore went to other sources for help and tried to rationalize my problems. But through these processes of logical reasoning, I soon found my Bible fast becoming explained away rather than explained. I was left mystified, unsatisfied.

In my dilemma I did finally come to Aunt Verna. Very simply and graciously she explained to me the verse that says, "The natural man receiveth not the things of the Spirit. . . . because they are spiritually discerned." This proved to be the golden key for me that unlocked the door to the things of the Spirit.

My struggle between natural concepts and spiritual revelation was further resolved by an experience I had while in training with the United States Naval Air Corps.

It was my first instrument instruction flight. We were at seven thousand feet when my instructor barked back over the intercom, "All set, cadet; safetybelt secure, hood closed."

"All set," I replied, as I pulled the hood over my rear cockpit, shutting from sight all outside mediums of orientation. I squared myself in my seat, determined to make a success of my first blind flight.

Then things began to happen, fast!

First, I felt the nose of the plane plunge earthward. The next moment I was squeezed down into my seat as the ship headed for the clouds again. Then, with a burst of added power, I felt myself hurled forcibly to one side of the cockpit as my instructor evidently applied full rudder. I was hanging in midair by my safety belt. And at this exciting moment, my instructor shouted back, "Okay, you've got it!" I felt the control stick go limp; the ship was mine.

In one of these brief seconds that seems an age, I tried to analyze what had happened: first a dive, then a climb, a skid to the right, and now I was hanging upside-down by my safety belt. Simple, I thought, nothing to do but to pull back on the stick and bring us around to our original upright position, thus completing the loop; both airspeed and altitude would become steady again as soon as we would come around into normal position.

But the airspeed and the altitude did not become steady. Instead, faster and faster, and down and down we went. I pulled back hard on the control stick. Cold sweat broke out over my body. I tried to reason out the situation. Had the control cables snapped? I jiggled the stick. There was response. What, then, could it be?

Suddenly, as though audibly spoken by someone at my side, the words of my ground instructor came to mind. "Remember," he had said in his last class period, "ignore your own feelings; believe the instruments; believe the instruments!"

The instruments! O yes, the instruments! Let's see, airspeed now 120 mph; altitude now under three thousand—and then I saw it, *the turn and bank indicator!* Sure enough, the needle was clear over to one side, showing that we were in a steep bank. In the nick of time I "believed the instrument" and pulled out of my predicament. Had I continued to trust my own judgment, I would have continued in my "graveyard spiral," ending up on the ground in a burst of flames.

And then I thought, in matters pertaining to life and faith, have I not been flying blindly, trusting to human reasoning and natural inclinations, following ways that *seemed* right to me, instead of "believing the instruments?" In my self-sufficiency and pride I figured out the answer, and the answer was wrong. And all the while God's infallible instrument, His Holy Word, was telling me plainly how to come out of the death spiral. Here was Aunt Verna's secret in beautiful Christian living; she was flying by instrument.

I began to give attention to the Instrument. God's Word showed that I was lost. I knew that. At least I knew that something was seriously wrong; I knew that I was a sinner. And the Indicator said, "Behold the Lamb of God that taketh away the sin of the world!" "Believe on the Lord Jesus Christ and thou shalt be saved." And I did believe on Christ. I quit my reasonings, believed the Instrument, and pulled out of my spiritual spiral.

Thus did I discover the Bible to be a *revelation* and not a treatise or a code of ethics; it is "the power of God unto salvation." Man can not hope to thread his intellectual way through complex mazes of cultural and scientific truth. God sees all the angles, and He offers to man *Ultimate Truth,* and asks that man believe the Truth, so that the Truth can "make him free."

And thus have I averted the fatal fiery finish of a graveyard spiral. I have headed my plane into the clouds and through Aunt Verna's secret of spiritual discernment now enjoy the sunshine and joy of the infinite expanses of God's redeeming and keeping grace.

* * *

26   A CONVERSION; A TESTIMONY; A SONG

Virgil P. Brock and his wife, Blanche Kerr Brock, are co-authors of many of the gospel songs used by evangelical churches. "Sing and Smile and Pray" and "Beyond the Sunset" are samples. Evangelist Brock here tells how one of their best known productions came to be written. It is quite fitting that these writers of gospel songs should have their residence at one of the great centers of gospel preaching in America—Winona Lake, Indiana.

An unusual experience in soul-winning early in our evangelistic ministry, was the one associated with the writing of "He's a Wonderful Savior to Me."

I had gone into a business place to talk with the owner about his becoming a Christian. I found him listening intently to something that a traveling salesman was saying. Moving closer, I caught the drift of the conversation. "I'd rather see you become a Christian," said the salesman, "than to sell you a big order of goods."

Stepping over to the side of the business man, I introduced myself. "I do not know this man," I said, indicating the Christian salesman, "but I see from the button on his coat that he is a Gideon, and I know you appreciate his interest in you. If you believe what he is telling you, why do you not make the decision *now?*"

Very simply the business man did there make his decision. After we had together bowed our heads in a prayer of thanksgiving, he left immediately to tell his family what had happened.

That evening the business man brought his wife and his two teen-age children to church. He brought them not only to church, but also to Christ. They had come early, and when the opportunity was given, all made public confession of Christ. Later they were baptized.

I had asked my Gideon brother to give his own testimoney at the same evening service. He related how he had been saved from a sinful life during a drunken debauch in a hotel room through the prayers and instruction of still another Christian traveling man. In the course of his testimony he used the phrase, "He's a wonderful Savior to me," over and over again.

The night following that blessed service I awoke about four o'clock to find myself singing the chorus of "He's a Wonderful Savior to Me." This awakened Mrs. Brock. I urged her to dress and go to the hotel parlor and play it. She did. And in that early morning hour was born a song. Truly, "He giveth songs in the night!"

* * *

27   **A SCIENTIST FOR CHRIST**

Millions have seen the "Sermons from Science" films produced by the Moody Institute of Science. Superb in technical photography and accurate in scientific detail, these productions have achieved renown in both scientific and religious circles. Unbelief and resistance to the claims of Christ must give way for the person who with an open mind views such films as "The God of Creation," "Voice of the Deep," and "Dust and Destiny." George E. Speake is an associate with Irwin A. Moon in the production of these films.

I was born and raised on the East Coast, living in Baltimore, Washington, New York and, finally, in Philadelphia. My parents were Christians and brought me up to attend church and Sunday school. When I was ten years old I joined a church in Philadelphia at the same time the rest of my family did. I have no conscious memory of any conviction of sin or any need of a Savior at that time. However, I faithfully attended church because of the many friends I had there.

When I started to college at the University of Pennsylvania, in the engineering school, I drifted further and further away from church activities. I was not openly rebellious, but just not interested or attracted.

I went to church out of respect for my parents; I attended Sunday School because attendance was necessary to play on the basketball team; I went to young people's in order to get a date. Such was the depth of my spiritual life in my first two years in college.

However, by the grace of God I became acquainted with a group of young people who really loved the Lord and had a genuine testimony of the reality of a life in Christ. In a wonderful way about the same time I began to think of the emptiness of mere physical existence. Many of the young people could speak with certainty of the eternal life they had in Christ, of the promise of heaven, of a sweet, abiding peace, and of a purpose in living for Christ and His service. Although I could lead in public prayer and possibly take part in some religious programs, deep down in my heart I knew that I did not *know* the Christ that these others spoke of.

Finally, when I was a junior in college, on November 18, 1934, at a service in Philadelphia at the West Branch Christian Endeavor where Rev. Doug Roe was speaking, the Lord saw fit to save me. The best I knew how, I received Christ as my Savior, and since that date He has been real to me.

As a testimony to Matthew 6:38 I would like to tell of the blessing I enjoyed when I put "first things first." Up until that time I had been struggling along with my college work, just barely getting by. But now, by the end of the junior year I was on the honor roll, and upon graduation in 1936 was awarded the Senior Mechanical Engineering prize at the University of Pennsylvania.

During the War I rose through the ranks to the position of Air Officer on the flagship carrier in the

Pacific, for which I was awarded the Bronze Special Navy Unit Commendation.

After the War, I wanted to invest my engineering and technical experience and education in the Lord's service. He has now permitted me to be associated with the Moody Institute of Science in the great project of preaching the gospel story through the medium of scientific films. I now have a sweet Christian wife and a little boy five years old.

For me there is nothing the world has to offer that gives the joy of serving Christ; Philippians 1:20, 21 is verified in my life.

* * *

28   AN INTERDENOMINATIONAL CONVERSION

It is only natural that Dr. Paul W. Rood should have supported a world-wide evangelical movement like the Youth for Christ International. It was at the Congress in Brussels, Belgium, where Dr. Rood was one of the principal speakers, that he handed the compiler this story of his spiritual birth. Dr. Rood was president of the World Christian Fundamentals Association.

When I was fourteen years of age I worked in a factory in Portland, Oregon. A young man who also was employed in this factory, spoke to me one day about the Lord. He had been saved the night before and immediately started to witness for his Savior. He asked me if I was a Christian. I answered affirmatively. Then he asked if I was born again, and to that pointed question I had to answer no. His comment was that if I was not born again I was not a Christian.

That noon we ate our lunch together. My friend read a chapter from the Bible. By this chapter I was brought under deep, pungent conviction of sin. This started me to read the Bible still more and to pray; but for some reason I could not find peace.

One day in my reading I came to the passage in Matthew 10:32, 33: "Whosoever therefore shall confess Me before men, him will I confess also before my Father which is in heaven. But whosoever shall deny me before men, him will I also deny before my Father which is in heaven." This caused me to realize that I must publicly confess Christ before I could receive assurance. This truth is also brought out clearly in Romans 10:9: "That if thou shalt confess with thy mouth the Lord Jesus, and shalt believe in thine heart that God hath raised him from the dead, thou shalt be saved."

I made my way to a union campaign service conducted in a neighboring Baptist church. The evangelist was a Presbyterian. When the invitation was given, the Holy Spirit spoke very definitely to me saying, "This is your last opportunity." I made up my mind that if someone would speak to me, I would tell him about my need and longing.

"Are you saved?" asked a young man as he approached me. I knew God had sent him, and I said, "No; but I would like to be." I followed him to the front of the church where he turned me over to a Methodist preacher. This understanding preacher asked me to tell him about my need. I said that I had been reading my Bible for a whole month but that I could not get any light or peace in my heart. "My boy," he answered, "remember what Jesus said"; and he quoted John 6:37, "Him that cometh to Me I will in no wise cast out." As he repeated those words the burden fell from my shoulders, the peace of God came into my heart, and the joybells commenced to ring. There was a new name written down in heaven, and it was mine!

On the way home that night I knelt down on the street and thanked God that I was saved. I was that happy. Shortly afterward I had the opportunity of giving my testimony in a Salvation Army street meeting.

Thus it was that I was led to the Lord by a Methodist preacher following a message by a Presbyterian evangelist in a Baptist church, and gave my first testimony in a Salvation Army street meeting. It is not surprising therefore that I am giving myself to interdenominational work in the Bible teaching and evangelistic field.

I thank God that I was saved as a boy, and that I have had the privilege of serving my Lord and Savior ever since that memorable day when He spoke peace to my soul.

* * *

29   SURE CURE FOR ALCOHOLICS

Out of the files of the American Soul Clinic, of Los Angeles, California, comes this "fresh-from-the-oven" conversion story, narrated by Fred Jordan, founder and head of this soul-saving organization.

"Come in," he said.

"I can't; the door is locked," I replied.

"O.K.! O.K.!! O.K.!!!" he impatiently mumbled and drawled, for he was drunk, very drunk.

The snap of the Yale lock ended a tedious pause. The door opened—and there he was, doubled nearly to the floor, trying to wind his way back to the foot of the bed. Reaching the bed, he slipped and fell flat.

I noticed a little capsule in his bed, and slipped it into my pocket; you see, I wanted him to have another chance, and not to commit suicide.

"You're Fred Jordan, aren't you?" he stupidly observed as I lifted him into his bed. "Can't you help me?" he continued. "I've been drinking for fifty-one years." Tears stood in his eyes.

"But drinking is still sin, and Christ died to save sinners from their sins, and I want to put my hands on you now and ask the Lord Jesus Christ to send the demon back to hell," I said. "You must have help to-night."

Then I prayed for the deliverance of this man from both the guilt of sin and its enslaving power. I prayed that God would sober him and make him to realize his need.

I promised to come to him again the next day.

"Will he be dead? Will he be sober? Will I find him in his room? . . . ."—these were the questionings in my mind as I climbed to his room early the following morning.

No sooner had I opened the door—it was unlocked this time—than I realized that God had answered my prayer, for the first words that greeted my ear were a sane and cheerful "Hello, Fred!" He was wearing clean pajamas and his mind was fully rational. Because he

had not eaten for three days, I took him out to breakfast, and then to my home.

That same evening, Charlie Baldauf—for that was
the alcoholic's name—stood at the microphone of the
American Soul Clinic's daily broadcast and gave his
testimony of what had happened that day.

"I want to thank the Lord for giving me another
chance," he said. "This morning my sins were heavy
upon my heart. All at once the Lord picked me up out
of the gutter, and now my sins are all on Him. Many
times before I had tried to live a Christian life in my
own strength, but I failed over and over again. I want
to thank and praise the Lord for everybody who has
been praying for me in answer to Brother Jordan's
request over the radio last night. I thank You, Lord,
and give *You* all the credit."

Twenty-four hours later, Charlie Baldauf again stood
at the microphone. "I want to thank all you folks again
for your prayers, and I want to tell you that the Lord
has saved me and that last night I could not sleep for
joy. I didn't want to sleep. I was so happy, and I'm
still so happy today. He is such a wonderful Savior.
He even gave me a chance to testify for the first time
in my life. When I went to the hotel today for my
clothes, I gave a tract to the maid, and she invited me
to talk and pray with her. Two of the boys came up
after me and we three went down and prayed for the
lady. From now on I want to work for the Lord."

Twenty-four hours still later found Charlie reconciled
and reunited with his wife. The climax came when the
three of us bowed in a prayer of thanksgiving and
praise for a Savior who can forgive the sins and break

the chains of a fifty-one-year-long alcoholic and can reinstate him in loving fellowship with both God and wife. It was a hallelujah prayer meeting.

* * *

30   T-H' W-I-N-N-A-H DOES NOT ALWAYS WIN

"Sailor" Eddie Huffman, former all-Navy light heavy-weight champion, gave his testimony at the Church of the Open Door in Los Angeles that he did not know what conquering really meant until he learned the secret of Romans 8:37, "We are more than conquerors through Him that loved us."

Many times I have heard the plaudits and the shouts of the crowds urging me on to victory; many times I have left a fight arena with a victory to my credit and with thousands of dollars to add to my bank account. According to the world's way of thinking I should have been a very happy boy. But little was it realized by my shipmates on the USS Mississippi and by the many thousands of friends and fight fans throughout the country who cheered me from one victory to another, that I was in reality a defeated man, rather than a victor. How little the world knows of the heart's longing!

Money and fame alone will not give peace to the heart. I have had both, and they never give rest to the inward man.

The records show that I never lost a fight in the Navy while climbing the fistic ladder to the "All-Navy Belt." I made tens of thousands of dollars in the prize rings of the nation as I fought and defeated "top notch" fighters.

I have heard the roar of the multitudes as victory was acclaimed in prize fight fashion time after time, but only God knew how empty it all was. The throngs shouted; the press emblazoned the news of "The Sailor —Th' Winnah"; and for the moment I sensed the flush of victory; yet it all seemed so much in vain. The cry of my heart was never silenced nor was the inward longing ever satisfied. I suffered periods of depression in spirit which I could not understand at the time. It is all so very plain now, for I know that "Man does not live by bread alone." With all the praise and plaudits of the crowd, I knew that deep within I had no peace of heart or mind.

My wife, Mabel, and I often talked about God and we would pray before each "bout." We would often send money to a church, thinking that possibly this act of giving might help us in some mysterious way. In other words, we were trying to *buy* peace and rest of heart and mind.

On August 28, 1934, six years after leaving the ring, in need of money—for the dollars had slipped all too quickly through my careless fingers—, I found myself walking the streets of Long Beach, California, in great discouragement. My home bid fair to crash on the rocks that line the shores of sin. My drinking and gambling had broken the heart of my wife, and she threatened to leave me if I did not change.

On this particular day I was recovering from an orgy of drinking when there was handed to me a book entitled, *From Crime to Christ*. After some hesitancy, I opened the book and read about Dan McNally, alias

Joe Kenny, No. 19294. This man was an ex-convict from the Missouri State Penitentiary. It was a remarkable story of deliverance from sin through faith in Christ. The story deeply impressed me and I resolved to hear his testimony from his own lips. That evening I suggested to Mabel that we go to Dan's mission in Los Angeles.

I shall never forget the impression I received there. "Blood-washed men," though ill-clad and destitute of this world's wealth, stood to their feet, and with a light in their faces, told how Christ had redeemed them. As I listened, I said to myself, "If Jesus Christ can save these men, surely He can save me too." Without telling my wife, I lifted my heart to God and Prayed: "O God, if you can save these men you can surely save me, and I pray you for Christ's sake to have mercy on me and save me right now."

Immediately a change took place within me. A heavy burden was taken away, and I felt my heart grow light. At that moment I was saved through faith in Jesus Christ. I have never again experienced the old sense of bondage.

In the following morning service, to the great surprise of my wife, I rose and made my first public confession of Christ as my Savior. Mabel was quick to follow, and we both found a joy that we had never known before.

Humble submission to the will of God brings supreme happiness, something that the "husks" of the world can never give. All praise for this belongs to my Lord and Savior Jesus Christ.

139

On January 3, 1937, Dr. Walter Manuel Montano, known as Fray Luis, knelt in the prayer room of an evangelical mission in Cuzco, Peru, and rose a born-again Christian with a burning desire to see the gospel preached throughout the continent of his birth, South America. Head of the Western Hemisphere Evangelical Union, Dr. Montano is today a great moving force for Evangelical Christianity in South America. He is the famous "Monk Who Lived Again" in the book by that title, now in its eighth edition (Light and Life Press, Winona Lake, Indiana). The following story of his conversion is an adaptation of a series of articles appearing in the "Sunday School Times" in 1947. Used by permission of the "Sunday School Times" and of Dr. Montano.

In a special festival in honor of the Virgin Mary, in the month of March, 1920, I began my religious life as a novitiate in the Dominican Order of the Roman Catholic Church in the city of Cuzco, Peru. I followed the very special and solemn ceremony, with the others who were beginning their lives as novitiates, and we walked to the little rooms that were assigned to us, where we were destined to spend hours, days, weeks, and months in solitude, meditation, and mortification of the flesh, interrupted by the community devotions in chapel and choir.

Every morning, at four o'clock, repeating the words, "*Benedicamus Domino,*" the priest in charge would call us. Between forty and fifty priests, all dressed in white robes with heads covered, would march to the choir through the dark halls of the monastery, repeating the *"Miserere."*

The period of probation finally passed, and, after examinations and the church's approval, I was admitted to Simple Religious Profession, which meant another special ceremony in the church and then my sacred promise to continue in the monastery for three years, observing the rules of holy poverty, holy chastity, and holy obedience.

Then, at the completion of those three years, I was approved for Solemn Religious Profession, the greatest event in the whole Order of the Dominican Monastery. At a fixed day, a great religious festival of the church, I was taken to the main altar. When the preliminaries were over and the sermon of the occasion was delivered, the high officers of the church being present, the Superior ordered me to lie down on the floor in front of the altar. I was covered with flowers in the presence of several thousand people and the Superior pronounced the sacred words, signifying my dying to the world and living for the church and the monastery and the defense of the faith.

I will never forget the deep impression that this ceremony left in my mind. I felt as if I had been transported in an ecstasy. I could hardly believe that I was the subject of all this great service and ceremony.

From the time that I entered the monastery, I was dedicated to study. The regulations of the Dominican Order read that if a Dominican friar forgets to study eight hours a day, he commits "mortal sin." Who would like to be guilty of that terrible sin? More than eight hours a day were spent in studies, such as Theology, by

St. Thomas Aquinas, in which we memorized every chapter of his twelve volumes written in Latin. Only those of us who were approved after serious and hard tests, as having earned a degree, were entitled to study directly in the *Summa Theologica* of Thomas Aquinas.

To conform with the strict discipline, the practice of the Solemn Vows, and to keep the almost permanent silence was not a difficult task for me. In fact, I enjoyed them—I found pleasure in them. But there was one thing that, like a termite, was little by little eating up all of that satisfaction, until I found myself with nothing but a shell. As a mortal being, I knew that sooner or later I had to die, but the terrifying thing was that I did not know where I was going to spend eternity. That thought created a kind of spiritual distortion in my soul that was the beginning of my spiritual pilgrimage. Thirsty and hungry, like a desperate soul in a desert, I went from experience to experience, looking for water, looking for bread, without being able to find the oasis.

Oh, how I tried to find some help! Oh, the nights that I would agonize, without being able to sleep! "Peace! Peace!" That was what I would cry in my dreams. "Peace! Peace!" That was the only thing that my soul was longing for. "Peace! Peace!" was what my heart was asking for. But, oh, how distant that peace was from me! My deepest devotion to the Virgin Mary and to some of the principal saints of the altars would not bring the remedy. Still determined to secure even a ray of peace, I turned to things that were not commonly practiced in the monastery, where, at the same time that we were observing strict discipline, we had every possible comfort for the flesh.

Sumptuous meals, abundance of the finest spiritous drinks, silk robes in summer, woolen ones in winter— poverty was practiced only in that no priest could handle money; but everything was provided for him, and whatever he earned went to the treasury of the monastery. Chastity was emphasized in that the priests cannot marry —but, oh, how many scandals were current because of the conduct of some friars! A father commissar, sent from Rome to investigate the moral conditions of the monastery, said to us at the end of his investigations: "The robes that you wear are white, but your hearts are as black as the smoke of hell." Obedience, of course, was paramount, until we all had to surrender our wills to the Superior's will.

But one can not enjoy any comforts if the soul has no peace. That turbulent and horrible spiritual torment was breaking my life to pieces. How could I have had joy in these human facilities for the body? Perhaps if my Superiors had suggested some kind of extra penitence, I should have been encouraged and accepted that penitence as a means of bringing calm to my spiritual distress. But no! On the contrary, one day, as I told the confessor that I wanted to practice some penances, he definitely ordered me not even to think of "that foolish idea." Nevertheless, I thought that God would be satisfied, and taking "that foolish idea" as my only chance to prove whether God could still be manifested through penances, regardless of the confessor's prohibition, I began to subject my body to sufferings in a way that nobody would discover.

Night after night, I used to remove the mattress from my bed and lie down on the bare springs. This would give my soul a momentary satisfaction, but that satisfaction would soon die. To make my penances harder and harder, when I was in the dining room, if the other priests were not looking at me, I would manage to put ashes or too much salt in my soup and eat my spoiled dinner as if it were a banquet. For a long time I wore a "cilicium," a kind of iron belt with sharp points that would torture me until my body was bleeding. And I was determined to go on in penances if they would bring me peace. But the peace I longed for never came.

Soon afterward, I was ordered to go from the city of Lima to the city of Cuzco, where among other things I was to teach church history to the students of the monastery, and perform other duties, especially that of "Mayor of the Students."

One day while I was in charge of a library, with the help of a lay brother I was dusting and arranging some of the books. At the end of the library was a small room called "Little Hell." All the condemned books—non-Catholic writings—were placed in that room. No one had access to them except with special permission of the Superior. The lay brother and I were in that section fixing the books in their respective places. Suddenly one of the books tipped from its position on the bookshelf, and as I put it back in place I saw the title—"Nights with the Romanists."

At first I did not pay much attention, but as I was going to the other bookshelves, that title stuck in my mind and my curiosity was aroused to see that book. I opened the first pages and I knew that book was condemned, that I was even committing a terrible sin by opening it. I promised myself that after reading the preface, I would put it back, but that only created an intense interest in the contents of the book. I looked at the lay brother—he was fixing other books, his back toward me. Making sure that he was not watching me, I put the book under my robe and then ordered him to close the library.

Impatiently I waited for the night. At half past nine the bell would ring with the special meaning to all of us: "Silence. Silence. Silence." The lights would be turned off, and the monastery would be covered with the darkness of night. Silence everywhere! Not a single movement! But I was anxious to read the book. Somehow I managed to take a candle and fix it so no reflection could be seen from without. I almost covered the candle with my blanket in bed, and read.

Night after night I would repeat that procedure. I was fighting. That book was like a human being. Reading the arguments, I would answer as if I were talking to a person. As if I were fighting with somebody, many times I would be tempted to throw the book from me.

But all of that did not help me to find peace. On the contrary, I was living in an awful tempest, disturbed until I was not able to sleep, even at night. I was compelled to read the book the second time.

One day during the silent hour at noon day, when all the priests were taking their siesta, I was reading in "Nights with the Romanists." No doubt I was tired, for as I was sitting in front of my desk, the opened book before me, gradually my head fell upon my hands, and I went to sleep. Suddenly, in what seemed to be a nightmare, I heard a noise; but it was a reality, for the Superior of the order was actually entering my room.

Calling me by the name I had taken upon entering the order, he said: "Father Luis, if you are so tired, why do you not have your siesta, instead of just sleeping with your head on the desk?" As the book lay open, he asked me what book I was reading. Terribly confused, I could not make a clear answer. He noticed that I was nervous. He came closer and closer, and took the book in his hands and read the title.

"A book from 'Little Hell'!" he exclaimed. "Why did you do it? I had appointed you to be in charge of the library because we all felt that you could be depended on and we trusted you. If it were the case of another priest who does not have your privileges, the punishment would be greater."

Then he told me what my punishment was to be. I had to kneel down in front of the Superior, kiss his hand, and accept the punishment. Day after day, at meal time, I had to lie down at the door of the refectory while all the priests had to step on my body. After the usual prayers, I would go to the center of the refectory to have my dinner or supper, and, kneeling down, would eat my meals from a piece of wood instead of a table. When the meal was over, I would go to the thirty-five or forty priests one by one, kissing their feet. The punishment came to an end, but the sores opened in my soul were deeper, not because of the punishment, but because of that horrible mental suffering; the peace and happiness that I expected to find in the monastery did not come to me.

My birthday was January 1, 1927, and, as was customary, it was celebrated in the large living room of the monastery. They all took part in that kind of festival, specially imported wines were served, and lots of things happened during this celebration. The night of January 2, after we finished repeating the prayers in the choir, the Superior indicated that there was quite a bit left from the previous night, so we were called back to the living room. No one could understand why I was not taking part in that celebration, although it was my own birthday. The Superior came to me with these words: "What is wrong with you? Why aren't you happy? Are you trying to spoil your own birthday party?"

I just fixed my eyes on the beautiful oriental rug and did not answer a word. As soon as he went to the other side, I managed to leave the living room and went to my own dormitory. In the secret of my thoughts I said goodby to the priests, to the choir, to the living room, and to the other places that were so familiar to me. I went to my dormitory with the determination to escape from the monastery. With that in mind, I packed my personal belongings.

At last, in a room near by, the alarm clock rang—it was four o'clock. The brother in charge of calling us to the choir went from door to door repeating, *"Benedicamus Domino."* When he stopped before my door, I managed to answer, *"Deo gratias."* Leaving the patio around which we had our dormitories, he went to the other sections of the monastery. Putting my shoes under my arm, and taking advantage of his having opened the door from one patio to another, I followed him at a distance without being heard or seen.

He passed the Superior's door and I had to pass the same way. But as I reached the Superior's door, one of my shoes fell to the floor. How terrified I was: "Will the Superior come out and find me? Will the brother realize, discover, and denounce me?"

Apparently no one heard, so picking up my shoe I went ahead. The greatest obstacle was before me, as the doors connecting the monastery to the church, the only way to go out to the street, were locked. The working man in charge of the keys had his room near the ancient temple of the Sun, built by the Incas, the very place in which the Dominican monastery is built today.

The priests began the morning prayers. They bowed their heads and remained a few minutes in silence. I knew every detail of these devotions. While they had their heads bowed, walking on tiptoe, I went to the big colonial door that opened to the street, underneath the choir. Pedro followed me. He was barefoot. That very minute, I said, "Pedro! This is the time. Use your key to open the door."

A few minutes later, I was going through the dark and narrow streets of that ancient city of the Incas, the city of Cuzco.

When I made up my mind to escape from the monastery, I knew exactly where I was going. It is true that I did not know any Protestant missionaries. My notions concerning Protestants were wrong. In spite of that, there was a certainty and an assurance in my heart that if I went to the Protestant mission I would be accepted. So with this thought, "If the Protestants worship evil spirits but have peace, I prefer to go with them," I went to the Protestant mission.

Just after four o'clock in the morning of January 3, 1927, I was knocking at the door of the mission. After a few minutes of waiting, an Indian gardener opened the door. He was shocked when he saw me there, dressed as a Dominican priest.

"Father," he said, opening his big eyes wide, "this is a Protestant place."

"I know that," I answered, and as I did not know what title to give the missionary, I asked the Indian gardener to call the chief.

He said that it was too early to disturb him. Consequently I waited, talking to the gardener and asking him question after question. Our voices were heard by the missionary, and, a few minutes later, a tall North American missionary was walking toward me.

There was kindness in his look, and his words were: "Is there anything I can do for you?" Shaking hands with him, looking into his eyes, I put my heart into my words: "Will you just answer my question? Do you have peace by being a Protestant? If you only knew what I am passing through, if you could read my heart, you would not deceive me. Will you answer just this question?"

That man, who hardly knew how to speak well my own language, Spanish, answered me in clear words: "You will excuse me if I do not begin this introduction with arguments, but I want to tell you that some time go I came to Christ as my Savior. I recognized my condition and my sinful nature, and as I came to Him as a sinner, He showed Himself to me as a Savior. He changed my life, and that is why I am here, to bring souls to the only Savior."

Without any further conversation, he kindly invited me to enter a little room. At about five o'clock that morning I saw him kneel down, and I followed him. He closed his eyes— I had my eyes open. I was observing everything he did. When he began to pray, it seemed to me he was talking to someone who was real, who was present.

His prayer was: "Lord, save this soul. Lord, give him peace. Reveal Thyself to him." As he continued praying, tears were rolling down his face. Then he asked me to pray, too. My answer was: "I do not know how to pray that way. I am not accustomed to that kind of prayer. I have not brought any of my books from the monastery."

That man of God said, "Your books will not help you. You just open your heart to God. Express your need to Him." So I began to pray more or less like this: "If God is here, He must know what I am passing through. If Thou art God, prove it by giving me peace. This is worse than hell." I was overcome with emotion and could not say any more words.

It was then that this missionary opened the Scriptures. When he read the passages, I said, "I know these passages." But somehow, familiar as I was with the passages, never before had I taken them in the way it was presented to me that morning. A new light and power were manifested in the Scriptures, and then we prayed some more.

When we stood up, it was only ten o'clock, but, during the five hours of prayer and reading the Scriptures, something happened in my life. The terror, the doubts, the uncertainty had gone forever. I knew that morning that Christ died for me. I knew that morning that He came to me. He established peace in my heart, and my name was written in the book of life of the Lamb of

God. Even if I had millions of tongues, I could not praise the Lord enough for what He did that morning. Oh, how blind I was before that time, trying to substitute my poor penances and worthless merits for Christ's finished work on Calvary. All was paid!

* * *

32 "HOLDING" THE TRURTH versus SPREADING THE TRUTH

Arnold Grunigen, Jr. is vice-chairman of the Christian Business Men's Committee International, an association of Christian business men's committees of evangelical faith whose purpose and aim is to make Christ known as Savior and Lord. Arnold Grunigen, Jr. stands as a representative of that large group of Christian men who spark so many local spiritual awakenings across the land.

I grew up in a Christian home. Its roots went deep. Family worship, church attendance and consistent Christian conduct were so insisted upon and taken for granted that the spiritual atmosphere of the home was not regarded as unusual. My parents were both born in Switzerland and they never deviated from their path of Christian duty. They did not only show the way; they led the way. They invited Christians and Christian workers to our home repeatedly. Humble circumstances and a meagre table never stood in the way of an open house. The atmosphere was always charged with the power of God.

Small wonder then that such a home should let its imprint on one's character; small wonder that at the tender age of ten I knew the Lord as my personal Savior; small wonder that at the age of eleven I preached my first sermon to my father and mother and baby sister.

Came nineteen years of age and a crisis. Early in life I became acquainted with the investment security business (I'm still in it thirty-five years later!). This business is an active, virile, kaleidoscopic affair, and stood in sharp contrast to the comparatively static Christian surroundings. The Christian teachings were sound and true and biblical, but they were very dead. The saints seemed bent on "holding" the Truth, whereas I wanted to spread it. There just was too much difference in these two spheres of my life; something had to happen, for I was unhappy and almost morose.

At the right time the Lord provided an answer.

A full-time Christian worker came into our home. He was led to launch a city-wide interdenominational Christian witness in the heart of the business section in San Francisco, and he invited me as a young businessman to join the organization, acting as treasurer. I replied that by the help of God I would.

Then ensued two breath-takng years that called for courage and work and sweat and tears. I made contacts with many Christian leaders across the land. Will I ever forget my first street meeting? and the first evening I shared the platform with another missionary? Since those first experiences I have had many opportunities for a Christian witness in my work with banks and institutions and individual investors. This during the day. And then the evenings spent at the City Tabernacle in San Francisco!

And these two years were just the beginning; they laid the groundwork for the scores of subsequent major and minor roles that call for the testimony of the Christian businessman: on official boards of summer conferences; in developing wide-awake men's clubs; and, finally, in the unparalleled opportunity of the Christian Business Men's Committee International, with its numerous branches across the nation!

Truly God has made the business of Christian witnessing just as exciting as the investment security business!

* * *

33   I WAS IN REVOLT

Pioneer in radio and television religious broadcasting, Dr. Percy Crawford has at one time or other been guest in millions of American homes. His "Youth on the March" program is heard and seen weekly, his Pinebrook Young People's Camp draws thousands each summer, his King's College educates and trains for Christian service. Uncounted individuals over the whole world have found Christ as Savior through the multi-channelled efforts of this versatile and zealous Crusader for Souls. He tells here how he himself found the Lord.

In my youth I cared little for religious things. My father and mother were professing Christians. They compelled my two brothers and me to go to church (for which I am now thankful). My dad was a blacksmith who ruled his home with an iron hand, or, more properly, with a rawhide whip. So I went to church and Sunday School and even received a Bible for regular attendance.

But down in my heart there was revolt. I thought, You just wait; some day I'll grow up and I'll show what I'll do with your dry religion.

The time came when I had to leave school to go to work.

I got a job driving a fast delivery truck for a wholesale hardware firm. At the end of the first week I came home with a total of $23.50 for my pay. I thought I was a millionaire, and that my chance had now come. I waited until Mother was alone in the kitchen. Then I handed her some money and said, "Mother, I'll give you ten dollars a week for my room and board, and if you don't mind I'll do what I want about going to church.

After that my seat in church was usually empty.

My parents said, "Don't ever let us catch you with a cigarette in your mouth." So I started to smoke. My parents said, "Don't ever let us catch you in a pool hall." So I started to play pool and to gamble. My parents said, "Don't ever let us catch you in a dance hall." So I took dancing lessons. Many a night I had to climb a pole outside to the back porch and to my bed so that no one would know how late I got in. I was in revolt. I did not want religion; I wanted something with life and pep in it. I wanted to have a good time.

While still in my teens, I "went West" and drifted around awhile on the Pacific coast. In Portland, Oregon, I worked my way through High School, and then went down to Los Angeles by boat. During these years I was still in open rebellion against God.

Going down Broadway with my two suitcases in hand, I met two young ladies with whom I had been dancing on the boat. "Haven't you got a room yet?" they asked.

"No," I replied.

"Well," they said, "why don't you try the Bible Institute? There's a hotel for men there."

I thought, "Bible Institute!" Although the idea did not appeal to me, they did persuade me to try it. So in I went, set my two suitcases down in the lobby, walked over to the desk and asked for a room.

The man at the desk looked at me and said, "Young man, are you a Christian?"

Well, I had not come to be interviewed. Besides, I was no heathen. And since I thought I was a good deal better than many Christians I knew, I said that I was a Christian. I thought that because I had not killed anyone or held up a bank I was entitled to call myself a Christian. He gave me a room. That was Thursday.

That same evening I went to a dance; on Friday, I went to a party; on Saturday, I went to the Cinderella Roof Dance Hall, two blocks away from the Institute. On Sunday morning I thought it would be the thing to do to go to church. Dr. R. A. Torrey was then pastor of the Church of the Open Door. It is a large church, seating over four thousand, and I knew no one would recognize me. I sat fairly near the door just in case I did not like the preacher. Rev. William P. Nicholson preached that Sunday morning in the place of Dr. Torrey.

And did he preach! I never heard anything like it in all my life. I was used to a nice, sweet, soothing voice. I was used to poetry and book reviews and I could sleep well under that kind of sermon. But there was no sleep for me that morning.

Rev. Nicholson seemed to pick me out of that huge congregation and to speak directly to me. He preached on hell and heaven and sin and Christ and he told me

that Christ was the One I needed. God knows I was at
the crisis, the crossroads. God knows that I had to de-
cide that morning to go on one hundred per cent for
the devil, or to take my stand one hundred per cent for
Christ.

In the invitation that morning, I raised my hand, but
took it down quickly so that no one would see it. Then
when they sang a song and invited those who raised their
hands to go forward, I refused for a while, until a converted Jew came to me, put his arm around me and together we walked up to the front.

That was on September 23, 1923. That was my spiritual birthday, and since that day, the Lord Jesus has
given me an unbelievably deep and abiding joy.

It is because of this deep and abiding joy that I am
now a preacher. It is why I travel forty thousand miles
a year preaching the gospel. I long that other young
men and women, fellows and girls, may not let anything
keep them away from the Son of God. I long that they
may know HIM, whom to know is life eternal.

I guarantee that He can do for you, reader, what He
has done for me.

* * *

34   THE CROSS AT THE CROSSROADS

*Instrumental in establishing Christian colleges and
Christian printing presses in the Far East, Fred Jarvis is
currently on loan by the Evangelical Alliance Mission to
Youth for Christ International as Vice-President at
Large. He has been war correspondent in Korea for the
United Nations, is at present foreign correspondent for
Christian Life. Both before and after the Tokyo World*

Congress on Evangelism Jarvis has worked and prayed
for revival in the Orient. He conducts a weekly radio
broadcast in the States.

The single Christian influence of my childhood days ended with the early passing of my saintly mother. The most vivid memories I have of my father were the times he spent at home between jail terms. In my childhood and through my teens I knew nothing but the influences of a godless home.

Smoking at the age of nine; drunk at ten; playing hookey and carousing; fighting with father and brother, sometimes to the drawing of blood; stealing and pawning cars and jewelry and watches with my jailbird cousin; schooled in habits of sin and degradation by a man twice my age who was living in our house—these are my memories of childhood and youth.

My father did once make a feeble effort at a better life. "I am a widower and live alone with my two sons," he wrote in 1921 in response to a North Shore Church radio broadcast in Chicago. "Your broadcast brings back memories of sorrow and sadness to my heart. You see I am not a Christian. Neither are my boys. My wife was a beautiful Christian woman, but she died eight years ago. I am without hope and peace in the world. I request prayer of you people for my sons and for myself. We need them. From a sad but sinful heart . . ."

I am sad to say that my father never went farther than this statement of regrets. He continued in his life of sin and bad example until he finally died in an insane asylum from a dreaded social disease, the results of his own sins. It was not until I had been on the foreign mission field for several years that my father, in his last rational moments, confessed Christ as his Savior. He became a saved soul, but had to look back regretfully on a wicked and wasted life.

"Foreign mission field!" you exclaim incredulously? "How can a foreign missionary come out of such a godless home as you describe?"

Reader, I knew you would ask that question. I have wanted you to ask it. That God should pick up a boy from the gutter and send him to the uttermost parts of the earth is a miracle of Grace, and I want to tell you about it.

At the cross-streets of Van Buren and Western avenues in Chicago, on Monday evening, September 15, 1930, I came simultaneously upon another kind of crossroads, the most important crisis of my life. As I was transferring from one street car to another, a group of young people on the street corner caught my attention. One of them, a blond youth of about twenty, was preaching. I paused to listen. Then others testified to knowing the true way of life, the way of hope and happiness and peace. Something took hold on me. As I looked into the pure countenances of these young people—all of them about my own age—, I *knew* they had something that I lacked; their radiant faces contrasted so painfully with my sinful and songless soul. I listened on; street car after street car went by until my transfer ticket was voided, so absorbed had I become in the good news I was hearing. And it was taking on such a personal meaning; this good news had something to do with *me!* I listened on. Now a sense of sin pressed me down. But hope was born. I saw a way out; I would empty out my heartful of sin and ask the Savior to come in! I really would!!

158

And there at Van Buren and Western, cross-streets in Chicago where mill a million souls every day, I did just that. And something happened! Don't ask me how; I just know it happened. Heaviness left me and joy came in. At the crossroads of my life I found the Cross of Christ, and the Cross brought joy. I took on the yoke of Christ and I found that His yoke is easy. I transferred from the street car called selfish desire to the street car that's going up higher. And when at last I did continue my journey home from Western and Van Buren, I saw no need to pay a fare, for it was as though I were riding on air. At home, I wiped tears of joy as I read the beautiful tracts that they had handed me. At last I found what I had been longing for.

I was now a Christian. It seemed to me as though God had reached down His hand and pulled me out of a big, deep hole. In gratitude I wanted to give the rest of my life in the service of Him who saved me. Since I had had only six months of high school, I saw ahead of me a long and hard road of training. But I was constrained by the love of God, and for six years I attended high school evenings while working daily in an office. After high school came college, university and seminary.

Along this training pathway a precious girl came into my life and became my wife, and then we tramped the academic hallways together. During these trying but thrilling years we prayed and played and prepared together, and four times we had the joy of being graduated together, hanging up our A. B., B. D., M. A., and Ph. D. degree sheepskins side by side on our apartment walls. Our little son was present at several of the commencement occasions.

Our training over, we set our faces towards China. And now for seven years it has been our joy to serve the Lord in China (until the Communists drove us out), in Japan, in Formosa and in Korea.

That is how a juvenile delinquent from a godless home came to be a foreign missionary. It is the Lord's doings; it is marvelous in our eyes. Who would have thought it possible that a teen-age criminal with jailbird relatives should ever have a major role in the establishment of Christian colleges in Formosa and Japan, and in the setting up of Christian literature presses in Japan, Korea, India and Portugal?

Most tragic of experiences since my conversion was the farewell scene with my father when we left for China. In our visit to him in the mental hospital he was able to recognize neither me nor my brother (now also a minister) nor our newborn baby boy; he was completely unaware of the presence of the little child we loved so much. How hard it was to leave my father, knowing that he would soon die in this institution.

As I left that hospital—and my father—one thought was uppermost: What if Torrey Johnson—for that is the name of the blond "young man on fire" whom I listened to at the street meeting—had not preached the Good News of the Grace of God? What if I had not met Christ and His Cross at the Chicago Crossroads? Maybe I would have continued to follow in the footsteps of my father and have come to a similar end!

* * *

35   **CHAIN REACTION**

Bob Pierce is founder and director of World Vision Incorporated, a missionary organization that sees world needs and does something about it. World Vision is both vocal and visual in its technique; eloquent pulpit appeals and powerful and realistic films stimulate to missionary action. Bob Pierce ventures visions of such proportions as make us ordinaries vassilate in the contemplation of them. World Vision is largely the measure of this man's faith. Here he tells how it all started.

I was saved at the age of eleven.

Up to that time I had been a pretty wild youngster. You see I had much opportunity to do as I wanted since my mother was an invalid and my father worked away from home in order to earn enough money to pay the medical expenses of my mother's illness. But even though she could not keep her eye on me, my godly mother kept me constantly surrounded by prayer; she was believing God to do what she herself was unable to do.

Her faith paid off. One evening we went to church together, I on my legs of eleven summers and she an invalid on a stretcher. I do not remember any part of the message the minister spoke that evening, but I definitely do know that God convicted me of my need of a Savior. That evening, at the age of eleven, I became keenly conscious of the burden of my sins. I bore my burden to the altar and there God for Christ's sake took away my sins and really transformed my life. When I went home I was vividly aware that I *was* changed.

In the weeks that followed, others, too, became aware of the change. "What happened; you are so different?" they said at school the following morning. One of the "different" things was that of my asking the teacher's forgiveness for the trouble her eleven-year-old prankster had caused her.

On Saturday the people in the streets of my home town heard about my conversion. I gave my testimony at a street meeting in front of the fifteen-cent store in response to the suggestion of the wise pastor of the church where I had been saved. Although I did not know any Bible verses, I did know that I was changed, and I told my neighbors so. I said I felt everybody ought to give his heart to Christ. This simple street-meeting testimony was the beginning of a chain reaction that was to reach down to the present day.

Several days after this public confession of my conversion, the grandson of the people who lived next door to us came to his grandparents' house, and we played together. We had just got started in our games when he turned to me and said, "You know, Bob, you're different." He said, "I heard you on the street last Saturday night. Something's happened to you. What happened to you?" I said, "Well, I got saved." He said, "Well, what does it mean to get saved?" I tried to tell him, but I did not have any theological education and I hadn't studied any Navigator course. I told him that I knew I was a sinner and that I wanted Jesus to save me. We played on for a while longer.

Two days later we were together again. And again he said, "You know, Bob, something's happened to you; you're different than you were." I remember we were in the grandmother's front room, his grandmother out in the kitchen, when Ralph—for that was my playmate's name —suddenly turned to me and said, "Bob, I want to get saved like you've been saved." He said, "I want to get saved right now; how do I do it?" Well, again, I did not know how to lead him to Christ, but I remembered that I had got on my knees. So I told him, "Get on your knees and we'll pray."

We pulled a chair out from under the dining room table, and Ralph got on his knees. I said, "Now tell Jesus you are a sinner." And he did. Everything I told him to do, he just did it. I said, "Now if you believe that God answers your prayer, *believe* that God forgives you your sins and makes you His child right now." And he did it.

About that time Ralph's grandmother came in. She said, "What are you boys doing?"

I'll never forget his answer. He looked up and said, "I'm getting saved!"

I know that a lot of theologians would say that these doings of us youngsters was a mockery, that it couldn't be real. "Here's an eleven-year-old boy," they would say, "who doesn't know the Scriptures; how can he be leading a soul to Christ?"

Well, the facts are that when we got up from our knees, Ralph said, "Now can I go to church with you next Sunday?" I said, "Sure you can." And he said, "Do you suppose I could be in the street meeting with you?" "Of course," I said. Sure enough, next Sunday he did go to church with me. And the week after that, the second time I gave my testimony on the street corner, he was with me.

Our two families moved apart shortly after these events. I am now 38 years old. Twenty-seven years have passed since I led this boy to Christ just one week after I myself was converted.

Now what has been the outcome? Did God really do something? Did it really mean anything for an eleven-year-old boy, just converted himself, without Scriptures to quote, to kneel by the side of another boy in a dining room and try to lead him to Christ?

I did not know the answer until about six months ago when I came to Fresno to speak to four thousand people in the city auditorium. Freshening up in my hotel room just before taking a taxi to keep my appointment, I was surprised to hear my phone ring and a voice which I did not recognize:

"Is this Bob Pierce who used to live on 103rd Street in Los Angeles?"

"It sure is," I replied.

"Do you remember a family by the name of Tolson?"

"I sure do," I said unhesitatingly.

"Well," said the voice, "I'm one of the Tolson boys."

"Are you Ralph; Ralph was the first person I led to Christ?"

"No," responded the voice, "I'm not Ralph; I'm Ralph's brother."

"Tell me," I urged, "what is Ralph doing?"

"Oh," said my unseen guest, "Ralph is a Christian business man in Los Angeles. He married a fine Christian girl from a devout Christian family; in fact, his oldest daughter is preparing for the mission field right now."

"Thank God!" I exclaimed, "Imagine that happening out of my trying to lead a soul to Christ when I was only eleven!"

"Oh-h-h," interrupted the voice, "but much more than that has happened. Because you led Ralph to Christ, I'm saved."

"What are you doing?" I broke in rudely.

"I'm pastor of the Nazarene Church here in Fresno."

"Praise God for that," I said. "What else has happened?"

"Well, after you led Ralph to Christ, I got saved, as I said, and then my sister Lois got saved, and Lois is now married to a Plymouth Brethren Bible teacher and preacher and they live and work for Christ out on the southside of Los Angeles."

"What happened to your parents?" I asked excitedly as the childhood scenes flashed across my memory screen.

"Because we children got saved, my father and mother got saved, and when they got saved, my grandfather and grandmother got converted, having lived next door to you." The voice, too, was excited.

"And what became of your baby brother who was crawling on the floor in diapers twenty-seven years ago?"

"Well," said the voice, "he got saved too, and he is now pastor of the Oswego Presbyterian church in the city of Portland."

"Do you mean to tell me that your whole family has been saved?"

And then, as though summarizing the whole picture, Ralph's brother said with evident joy, "Yes, Bob, as a result of your leading my brother to Christ, three generations of us—every single one of us in the three generations—is walking with Christ. Three of us are full-time in the ministry, mother and grandmother are living near the church where you were converted and are faithful followers of the Lord. Father and grandfather are both in heaven."

There was a pause—as though for the meaning of it all to sink in—, a hurried goodby, and a dash for the taxi that was to take me to the Fresno Auditorium. Do you wonder that I experienced an added inspiration as I spoke to my audience of four thousand that night?

Six times now God has sent me around the world to preach the Gospel. I have had many thrills in the Master's service. But I think there never will be a bigger miracle than the one God performed in my childhood days. Through no cleverness or powers of my own, without my knowing how, I gave a simple testimony on a street corner one week after my conversion, and God used that stammering testimony to set off a chain reaction, the details of which came so unexpectedly over the Fresno telephone.

What is more, it is thrilling to know that the chain reaction has no end; the effects are going out in ever-widening circles. Only eternity will reveal the total end result.

* * *

36 BIRTH AND GROWTH OF A SOUL

By Norman A. Wingert

She came to our Neighborhood Activities Center in Vienna early in our two years of relief work in Austria. She had just hitchhiked to Vienna from Paris, was putting up in a youth hostel in the Danubian city, and was, according to her statement, now giving private French lessons to some University students.

The girl of whom I write was twenty-four years old, Dutch, cultured, and so refined and feminine in her bearing that my wife and I remarked what a fine and exemplary companion she would be for our daughter whom we had left in the States.

But the Mona Lisa smile was covering up a hidden inner turbulence. Victim of a broken parental home in the middle of her teens, she had been floating over Europe in a world of journalism and art, and her contacts with modern philosophical and political theories and propaganda had so confused her that thoughts of suicide were not unwelcome. Indeed, the idea had become tempting, now that she had just run away from a long-standing and persistent marriage proposal in Paris by a world-famous artist much her senior and from the luxury such a proffered marriage implied. Thus it was that she had come to rope's end at just the time when Mrs. Wingert invited her to spend the Christmas holidays with us at our Vienna Neighborhood Center.

We were not at first aware of the crisis. We gratefully accepted her offer to help with the office typing and with language translations — she spoke German, French, English and Dutch fluently—but our unseeing eyes did not catch the terrific soul-struggles which were going on beneath the surface of a casual and cultured calm. Even her semi-explained missions downtown and her late returns at night we regarded as no especial concern of ours.

But the struggles were none-the-less real, and they were fierce. During her three weeks' stay, our guest, as she told us later, secretly read the complete works of Jean-Paul Sarte, the French Existentialist, in an effort to find the secret of life and happiness. She frequented the art galleries, the cinema, and became an habitue of the night spots. She drank from many fountains of learning and pleasure and experience, but the waters were salty and smarted her soul-sores and left her thirst unquenched.

But God never disappoints a sincerely seeking soul.

Unbeknown to us, our little lady became during those three weeks deeply impressed with the quiet, Christian atmosphere of the Center, with the personal attention she received, and with the gifts of food and clothing "in the Name of Christ." In a subsequent letter she wrote, "I'll never forget how I was received: 'Hello, come in, your bed is ready; first have your supper.' I remember my supper. It was one after a week of not much. My stomach was filled, but more important, my soul was touched somewhere. This unusual love without having to lie for it was something! Never was there anyone in my life who got up early and made my breakfast for me — little things, yes, but the love with which it was done made them big things. I have lived in many ways, but it was quite new to see this religious way of living every day. I was very emotioned to see this good life and to benefit from it myself."

And then God spoke to her through the testimonies of others. She read in a book of conversion stories how others who had been searching all their lives found the Lord. She sat in on the Bible Study Hour and listened to the messages in the Sunday services. Best of all, she started reading the New Testament. Gradually she began to grasp the meaning of God's wonderful Good News. As she said later, "God showed Himself to me; He opened my eyes and heart."

One day our "little lady of the thousand veils" (so named by Helga, one of our Austrian workers) remarked to my wife that she knew she was on the wrong road, and then added, "Today was the first time in my life that I felt I even dared to pray to God."

Several days later, during our evening devotions, the girl asked quite unexpectedly if she would be permitted to offer a prayer. Those present will not soon forget that prayer. "Oh God," she began softly, "I have been on the wrong road. I want to thank You for bringing me to this house so that I could find the right road. Thank You. Thank You for what these people have done for me. Thank You so much! Thank You!" The prayer was short, but utterly sincere. That day, according to her own testimony later, she became a new-born child of God; old things passed away, all things became new.

Next day she left us to go into Germany. A week later we received a letter from her. Said she, "I can not imagine myself to be so far away from my American mother and father who gave me a lovely, quiet home for weeks, and, most important, who helped me to find the Lord, to begin a new life, to put away all worldly things, and to change for the most wonderful life—a life with God! I did not know how much I was missing when I did not know Him. I have to be thankful every day, very shamefully. The more I meet people out of your world, the more I like your world—God's world."

In a later letter to Helga, the Dutch maid remarked concerning her experience, "From miserable reality I made a fancy; I though it would help me, so I started with one little lie. Then people came with questions, and more little lies followed, and it seemed so easy to lie. I continued until I just lived in one big lie. The truth was so far from me that I even could hardly re-

member it myself, and still now it seems difficult to me
to see myself as I am and who I am. The big mistake
I made was to forget about Someone who was watching
me, Someone who sees and knows everything, and that
one day I should have to appear in front of Him. In my
wrong way of living, I did not dare to take His name on
my lips. I was not able to find the way alone, and then
He gave His hand to me. I could take His hand or not!
I am so glad I took it." And then she added, "I don't
know why God is so good to me; it is much more than I
can earn. I know I can not be thankful enough."

Helga's reply is a gem, and I must not omit it. "Dear
little lady of the thousand veils, how happy I am to see
you in the light of the rising sun! Good morning to you!
At last you are awake and have opened your eyes. May
you brush the cobwebs and bathe in the Eternal Light.
You'll see lands you never saw before; the new wings
of your soul are open wide, and the love of God carries
you to the realms of peace. At this very moment I write
I see you on this way. Beware of the lovely perfume
from the flowers of death growing on the many side
paths! Why do you tremble whenever you pass them?
Their poison can not harm you anymore. It almost
killed you, but it did not succeed; you are immune now.
You must know that nothing can touch you as you drink
of the Source of true strength. Receiving your letter
was a great joy to me; one of the greatest joys I ever
had. Only you made one mistake; you are not to thank
me for anything. I did what I had to do. It was all the
work of God. Think what *He* did for you!"

The next letter to Helga is likewise a gem. "Dear
Helga: Every day I enjoy again to live my new life.

God shows me the way every time when a little doubt tries to come upon me. There is no more chance. I can say that I have changed radically. I really feel I have been born again. I know it. I don't tremble anymore when the perfume of the death-flowers from the side paths tries to stun me. I don't want to see them and I don't smell their perfume, I can assure you that, for God has shown me the way too clearly. When I thanked you in my last letter for the things you did for me, I did *not* make a mistake, for, besides thanking you, I thanked *Him first* for the life He gave me. Many of these new things He showed me through you, Helga, the new friend in my new life, my dear little teacher in the most important things in life. Do you see now that I am right when I thank you too, many, many times?"

Then one day an announcement came to Helga: "Dear Helga, it is the Lord who has taken me away from the godlessness that means death and has given life to me. That is why I am going to be baptized next Sunday, to go on a contract with our Lord, with the will to follow in His steps. It is wonderful that He has taken me into His grace and forgiven my sins, that He has suffered for my sins. Let us pray, dear, dear sister, that He will give us the strength to do our part in bringing others to Him."

After the baptism she wrote to us of her joy: "Yesterday was the day I was baptized in the Baptist church in Stuttgart. It is wonderful, dear Mrs. Wingert, to know now why the Lord sent me to Stuttgart, why you had to offer half a night of your sleep in thinking about what you were going to do with me. It is wonderful when I look backward upon the past three months how He has

taken care of me in every way. To receive His love is
so great! To know that we always may count on Him,
that He'll always help us and lead us; isn't that nice!
He did not only give me all the comfort I could have
wished myself—work, a room, a nice place to live—but
He has also given me friends who teach me about His
Word. He has also given me much time to meditate
about Him, and to be silent when He is there Himself to
teach me and to tell me about my mistakes every day,
since I am a very new 'baby' Christian."

The following letter shows her spiritual growth and
progress: "When I wrote you in an earlier letter about
'putting out all worldly things,' a little fight with these
devil-worldly things was turning in me that very moment.
For a few days I was afraid of losing God, but He took
the fear from me and recalled to me your words, 'It is
up to you.' And I heard Helga again when she said
with tears in her eyes, 'We do not need to fear if we
really believe in Him and *live with Him.*' I feel free
now. Every day I feel renewed, every day more and
more. I am glad that I can say now, 'I *know* my Lord.'
There is no more 'but', no more doubts. It is so simple.
Wrong influences from outside never more will have a
chance to enter. It is of no more importance to me that
friends I had will no longer be friends of mine. I think
when I return to Holland, none of them will be there.
But the most important thing is that I have my Big
Friend who does not leave me alone; a new Friend who
opened a new life to me in a new world, who will go
with me everywhere and as long as I want it so."

About a year after the conversion of our Dutch friend
she returned to her "home" in The Netherlands. En-

route, the car in which she was riding was badly wrecked, and she lay dangerously near death for several weeks. Regarding the three following months in a convalescent home in the Rheinland, she writes, "It was a very still and advantaging time for my spiritual life and for contact with God. I am so thankful He saved me from worse things and that I may be again healthy and well." Running true to Christian form, she returned to her mother with a deep concern that her mother might find too the joy and happiness and strength which she herself had found.

The next letter came from Switzerland. "I am in the Bible School at Beatenberg. I can't say anything else than that it is a heavenly place. It is really a great grace having this opportunity and of going into the depths of God's Word. Should I ever have known when I first came to your place what riches the Lord had in store for me! In the two months I have been here, the Lord has blessed me so much. It is such a wonder! I am remembering you in prayer. Yours because of Golgotha."

Tilly Schaap will now soon have completed her training for full-time Christian work. I called to see her at the Bible School on my return to the States. The Administration of the school state that she is one hundred per cent genuine in her Christian profession, and that she is making a deep impress on faculty and students alike.

In her last communication to us, Tilly writes: "With deepest joy from the Lord in my heart I just want to send you my warmest greetings in the name of Him who saved us and put us into His Righteousness," and closes with, "One of your children you brought to Jesus."

Thus another soul was born into the Kingdom of God's Dear Son, and thus did the new-born soul grow into its spiritual maturity.

* * *

37   **OF SUCH IS THE KINGDOM OF HEAVEN**

How refreshing is the springtime breath of an early conversion! This experience is contributed by Frances E. White, B.A., M.A., Assistant Professor of English at Wheaton College, Wheaton, Illinois.

> "O for a thousand tongues to sing
>   My dear Redeemer's praise,
> The glories of my God and King,
>   The triumphs of His grace!"

Often heart has rejoiced that childhood lips were taught to sing the glories of my King, and that mind and heart early were filled with stories from the precious Word of God.

Our home was and is a happy, joyous one; for the Lord Jesus has been the center of its very life. All five of us children, three girls and two boys, came to the Lord Jesus in simple, trusting faith while still in our youth, largely because of the prayers and consistent lives of devoted, God-fearing parents; and all of us are happy today in His glad service. Father, quiet, kindly, and steadfast, and Mother, cheerful, energetic, and courageous, even in adversity, have been a constant source of inspiration to their lively boys and girls.

Father was Sunday school superintendent for many years, and often he would talk to the children about allowing Jesus to come into their hearts. One of these talks, given on a Sunday when I was about four years of age, made an indelible impression upon my heart and mind. It was not until the Tuesday following, however, that I had thought through completely what he had said. That day at family worship after Father had prayed, I suddenly said that I wanted to pray too. And at that precious moment, the Lord Jesus became mine for all eternity.

A year or two later, Father returned to my room after he had tucked me in for the night, and said, "Frederick wants the Lord Jesus to come into his heart tonight." And that evening all of us prayed around little brother's bed.

Struggles and trials have come since those days, of course; but always when the enemy would come in like a flood, the Lord has lifted up a standard against him (Isaiah 59:19). Increasingly the Lord has become nearer and dearer as we have walked and talked together in the heat of the noontide and in the cool of the morning and evening; and increasingly there is gratitude that He came into my child's heart to abide so long ago.

Many happy afternoons were spent listening to Father read from *The Pilgrim's Progress*. The words of Mr. Standfast as he was about to cross the river have echoed and re-echoed in my soul; and I have desired to make them mine when I, too, shall approach that crossing.

". . . . . I have loved to hear my Lord spoken of; and wherever I have seen the print of his shoe in the earth, there I have coveted to set my foot too. His name has been to me a civet-box; yea, sweeter than all perfumes. His voice to me has been most sweet; and his countenance I have more desired than they that have most desired the light of the sun. His words I did use to gather for my food, and for antidotes against my faintings. He has held me, and hath kept me from my iniquities; yea, my steps have been strengthened in his way."

* * *

38   A CLEAN HANDKERCHIEF AND A ROW CLOSER TO THE FRONT

Dr. Don H. Householder is a household name on the West Coast. From his Los Angeles Trinity Methodist pulpit and from the halls of the Union Rescue Mission (largest rescue mission in the world) go forth his simple but powerful messages to seen and unseen audiences. In Dr. Householder is found scholarship and spiritual understanding. He has studied at Asbury College and the universities of Southern California, New York, and Columbia; yet skid row bums can grasp the meaning of his words.

I could have been saved when I was still sixteen, but because I was timid and hesitant by nature, I did not—like the majority of our town's five hundred population—go forward to the mourner's bench in our community revival. But I was under deep conviction, and I can still see myself walking home under the starry heavens after the last one of these meetings, covenanting with God that if He would spare my life I would give Him my heart at the next revival.

You see, I had the wrong impression that if one is to be saved it must be in a revival. Had I but known, I could have reached out and touched God there that night on my way home. In the words of Jacob, "Surely God was in that place, and I knew it not!"

But true to my vow, I faced the issue in the next revival six months later. It was an old-fashioned camp meeting in the hills of Ohio. Each night I would slip into our cottage and get a clean handkerchief and go one row of seats closer to the front. Blessed are ye when each night you get a clean handkerchief and go a row closer to the front; for I say unto you that something is going to happen!

It was the last Friday night of the campaign. The minister had preached to youth. In his earnest concern, he walked down the aisle, came back to where I was standing, reached out his hand, and said, "Young man, don't you want to make the start tonight?" I replied that I did, and I took the first step. The second step was easier, and the third still easier, so that I was nearly running by the time I got to the straw at the altar.

Now morally, I had been a good young man. I could have been a good Pharisee and boasted of what I had done and of what I had not done. I had had no bad habits, had lived a clean life, and had even taught a Sunday School class occasionally. But I knew that I was not a Christian.

There at that altar that night I became a Christian, instantaneously, by the operation of the Holy Spirit on my heart and life. I did not need anyone to tell me that I was saved. There was no emotional outburst, but there was a voice within my soul saying, "Praise the

Lord! Praise the Lord!" There was no doubt about it; I was a changed young man.

That night I knelt and prayed at my bedside. I began to read the Bible prayerfully. I possessed a new nature now that hungered for the things of God. A sense of mission and purpose was born in my heart, and it was not long afterward that I answered God's call to full-time service.

* * *

39   **ON SEATTLE'S OLD SKID ROAD**

Don Mallough "rang the bell" when he was saved at "The Four Corners of Confusion" on Seattle's Skid Road. So sweet were those inner joybells that he, and his wife, Darlene, have gone into the bell-ringing business for God. Together they ring and preach the gospel, are known as "The Mallough Bell Ringers."

It was a balmy summer evening and folk in all parts of the city were strolling along the sidewalks and sauntering through the parks. The intersection at Washington and Occidental Streets was so crowded with men that it was practically impossible for vehicular traffic to pass. Hundreds of poorly clothed men stood in large groups clogging that intersection, talking to one another and listening to self-styled public speakers and soapbox orators.

This was Seattle's infamous "Skid Road." This was the intersection referred to as "The Four Corners of Confusion." Here uninitiated eyes got their first vivid glimpse of "life's other side." Here tender hearts were moved to tears, and unappreciative persons were made more thankful for such comforts as they possessed.

For many years I had heard of the old Skid Road. Now I stood at its very core. Three of my close friends and I had come here prompted solely by curiosity. We had elbowed our way through the throng and were pushing and squirming from one spot to another so as not to miss anything that was going on.

What a mixed multitude this was! Some of these men could rightly be called fugitives from work. Others were professional panhandlers who lived in cheap hotels but frequented a better part of town when asking for a handout. No doubt some practiced petty thievery. Most of them, however, were drifters and human derelicts. They were there as victims of circumstances, or as those who, having no initiative, had allowed themselves to drift downward and were without the power of will to extricate themselves from such a life.

What a strange hodgepodge of theories fell on our ears! It was truly a babel. Each speaker was giving expression to his own brand of religion or politics. On one soapbox was a Communist advocating the overthrow of existing forms of government. Fifteen feet from him was another speaker, apparently just as earnest, championing some other revolutionary measure. A stone's throw away was a man using the soapbox for its original purpose; he was actually selling soap. From across the street could be heard the strains of the Salvation Army band. Standing all by himself was a gray-haired man with but few listeners. One could get neither heads nor tails of what he was attempting to say, but he was going at it just as vociferously as the rest. Here at one intersection were seven or eight different kinds of open air meetings going on at one time. Is it any wonder it is called "The Four Corners of Confusion."

Suddenly above the din we heard another voice. With many others we wormed our way through the crowd to find out what new thing this was. There, in the center of a ring, stood a twelve-year-old girl preaching the gospel of the Lord Jesus Christ. We stood perfectly still while songs were sung and testimonies given. Then came the final word of prayer and a general invitation to attend the service which was to commence immediately in an upstairs mission.

As our excursion was somewhat of a "lark" anyway, we decided to go to this strange church. We were greatly surprised to find so large an auditorium and to see practically every seat taken. With the exception of the Christian workers on the platform, the congregation was composed entirely of men. How they did sing! Testimonies to the saving grace of the Lord followed, and then came a Spirit-anointed sermon. As we wended our way homeward we laughed and joked about all we had seen. We felt it had been an interesting evening's entertainment.

I laughed with the rest, but somehow a seriousness stayed with me. I didn't fancy going to church, and yet there was an inward urge that took me back (secretly, of course) several times in the following weeks. Never did I make known, by word nor act, what was brewing in my heart.

One night at the mission a young man spoke to me about my soul's welfare. He pleaded with me to yield to Christ. Other Christian workers gathered around.

When they saw that their efforts seemed vain, they began to pray. Soon there was a circle of men around me, praying for my salvation. That moved me as nothing else did, and when one asked if I wanted to go to the prayer room I answered in the affirmative. I even broke into a run to get there. Then, falling on my knees at that old-fashioned "mourner's bench," I called on God for mercy.

Oh, what joy and ecstasy flooded my heart when I made an unreserved surrender to the Lord! What peace and bliss surged through my being with the knowledge of sins forgiven! Never had I been so happy. From this time forward there was a complete change in my ambitions, my aspirations, and my outlook on life. Vocational plans I had cherished were shattered. I gladly threw my life open to do the will of the Lord, whatever that would be. The desire to live for Christ became uppermost, and the old longings faded into oblivion. I had been turned about by the transforming power of God.

Years have passed since that memorable night, and the more I ponder over it the more I marvel at God's providences. I had been in many beautiful churches, but He saw fit to save me in this humble place. I had heard speakers by far more educated than those in this mission, but their simple words struck a chord in my heart. In any other place I could have found a better class of people with whom to share a pew. But God knew that I needed the same gospel that those derelicts of humanity needed. Every person, rich or poor, young or olds, needs exactly the same old-fashioned salvation. "For all have sinned, and come short of the glory of

God . . . being justified freely by His grace through the redemption that is in Christ Jesus."

How I do thank God that His message was being sounded forth on old Skid Road! Out of the chaos and bedlam at that spot I heard the good news of salvation. At "The Four Corners of Confusion" I was led out of my state of sinful confusion into fusion with the living Christ.